THE TUNNELLERS OF HOLZMINDEN

The track of the Holzminden Tunnel after being dug up.

THE TUNNELLERS

OF

HOLZMINDEN

(WITH A SIDE-ISSUE)

BY

H. G. DURNFORD, M.C., M.A.

FELLOW OF KING'S COLLEGE, CAMBRIDGE

SECOND EDITION

CAMBRIDGE
AT THE UNIVERSITY PRESS
1930

CAMBRIDGE
UNIVERSITY PRESS

University Printing House, Cambridge CB2 8BS, United Kingdom

Published in the United States of America by Cambridge University Press, New York

Cambridge University Press is part of the University of Cambridge.

It furthers the University's mission by disseminating knowledge in the pursuit of
education, learning and research at the highest international levels of excellence.

www.cambridge.org
Information on this title: www.cambridge.org/9781107636071

© Cambridge University Press 1930

First Edition 1920
Second Edition 1930
First published 1930
First paperback edition 2014

A catalogue record for this publication is available from the British Library

ISBN 978-1-107-63607-1 Paperback

TO

MY WIFE

PREFACE

ALMOST exactly two years ago, as I write these lines, the famous Holzminden Tunnel became history. Even then, when the sordid camp was still lending (and seemed likely to lend *in perpetuum*) its grey colour to every aspect of life, when sense of proportion was practically dormant and racial animosity intensified to the highest pitch, it was impossible to overlook the peculiar dramatic proprieties of the event. Some day, it was felt, this story might be fittingly told.

And in the retrospect the feeling remains unaltered. The harsh angles have softened: the tumult and the shouting have died away to the remoter cells of memory: Captain Niemeyer (of the Reserve) has departed—God knows where! His imperial master is dragging out an unhappy old age in exile. The British protagonists and walkers-on in the 9-months struggle have scattered to the ends of the Empire on their lawful occasions. Once in a blue moon perhaps they think of it and rub their eyes. The details are already vague. The whole of their prison existence seems absurdly far away.

But it is in the hope that they will care to follow with not uncritical interest the following plain unvarnished account of the Tunnel episode that I, a mere looker-on, have sorted out the threads and fitted the jumble together. If any think this an impertinence, may I plead that an ordinary stage hand may see more of the workings of a nine months run than the star performers? To them at any rate, protagonists, walkers- and lookers-on in the event, and their friends and relations I would address myself particularly. Through them alone can I hope to interest the British public in this simple tale of a strategically unimportant but highly successful side-show, in Germany, in the dog days of 1918.

I am indebted to one friend in particular for assistance in the true description of the actual Tunnel. He prefers to remain anonymous. Many others of my ex-fellow-prisoners have helped me in various ways. The design which is reproduced on the cover was drawn by Lieutenant Lockhead while in captivity at Stralsund and was intended to serve as a Christmas card; I am indebted to him for the loan of the block. To Messrs Blackwood I am obliged for permission to reprint the personal experiences contained in the final chapter.

H. G. DURNFORD

KING'S COLLEGE,
  CAMBRIDGE.
      24th July 1920.

PREFACE TO SECOND EDITION

I AM deeply gratified by my publishers' suggestion that this book should be reprinted. The plainness of the story must be its justification. It is subjective and carries no moral. It barely touches the battlefields, recounts no actual horrors and does not emphasise the spirit of good-bye to "all that." If it stresses the indignities of captivity as a legitimate setting for the main episode, it is free from animus against the German nation as a whole.

The text is but little altered. I have added a page or so to the concluding chapter as I have been sometimes asked as to what happened after I had crossed the Danish frontier.

I will no longer accord Walter Butler, who supplied me with all the particulars as to the actual Tunnel and in fact wrote most of Chapter VI, the anonymity which he at one time insisted on.

H. G. D.

CONTENTS

ILLUSTRATIONS AND PLANS

PROLOGUE

"B/112th will detail the liaison officer for the Group for to-morrow the 5th."

The Brigade orderly splashed in bearing the unwelcome message. I had just turned in. The never-to-be-forgotten fatal three days' downpour which had set in on the 31st July 1917 and had upset so many calculations had just stopped and we had enjoyed an afternoon and evening of bright sunshine and cloudless skies. The water in the dug-out, which had risen steadily in spite of temporary responses to our efforts with an old trench pump and a chain of buckets, was now gradually beginning to abate and the stretcher on which I slept was once more high and dry. Also I was due to go down to waggon-lines in two days' time, and life generally was taking on a less sombre hue.

It could afford to. Our six weeks in action in the Salient had been lived in an atmosphere of almost unrelieved gloom, an atmosphere—so we had come to believe—inalienable from the place itself.

One had come to realise what men had meant who in earlier days on the Somme—when all was said to be quiet at Ypres—had trekked south into the Valley of the Shadow of Death and remarked that "it was better than the Salient." Now we had seen for ourselves. It had not merely been the shelling and the fact that there was not a really safe spot, except in the very ramparts of the Eastern wall themselves, between

D.   1

Belgian Battery Corner and the front line. It had not merely been that the German gunners conveyed the impression that they were *aiming* at *you*, that they knew exactly where you were, and that they were doing it— had been doing it all along—more as a pleasure than as an allotted task. It had not been the fact that no fatigue or waggon-line party could set great hopes on returning scatheless from a job of work; nor that here hostile aeroplane observation seemed more acute than in other parts; nor again that rarely a night passed but one saw or heard of some shambles on a main traffic road. It was none of these things. The spirit of Ypres was abroad, impregnating those new to her. From the very morning when, accompanying a harassed, jumpy acting C.R.A. on his round of battery inspections, I had first seen her, I had felt the spell upon me. It was like grey skies and a wind in the east, the quintessence of sombreness. The intervals of quiet could not be called peace; they served only to intensify the solitude. The history of the place seemed to cast its stamp on those who sojourned in it.

We had come into action at the beginning of July. Our instructions had been to get "in" and camouflaged and registered and then wait for "the day," and that waiting had been sorely trying to the patience. It had been far worse than sitting on the Messines Ridge in June. We had been told we should be "silent," but we had fired steadily nevertheless, and this meant, of course, more ammunition and added risk of casualties amongst horses and men. It had meant having the men out of cover to shift the shells from their depôts to the gun-pits; and such things were considerations when we

A street in Ypres.

The Cloth Hall in 1917.

The Menin Gate of Ypres.

were losing men at the rate of about two a day and the stock of capable gunners and N.C.O.'s, depleted at Messines, was beginning to run dangerously low. "D" Battery on our immediate right had had an even worse time. Poor old "D." They were always getting the rough of it since Courcelette, and this time they had got it very rough indeed. They had had no cellar to put their gun-crews in and we had been unable to spare them a share in ours, so they had left emergency crews at the guns and worked them by nucleus shifts, the remainder sleeping a long way behind.

The preparations had dragged their slow course along, and we had gone on with our daily routine, never knowing what the next minute was not going to produce, unloading and storing the ammunition, and heaving a sigh of relief when the last pack-horse had discharged his daily load and that anxiety at least was off our shoulders for the day; checking the sights and aiming-posts, strengthening so far as we could the pits, watching and shepherding the men; gassed one night and on duty all the next and then gassed again the third—the deadly mustard fellow had just made his costly début; counting the leaden hours, congratulating ourselves each time that—our duty over—we made the dug-out door afresh; and ever and anon looking hopefully through the tattered screen which still served to shield our part of the Menin Road from hostile observation to where Passchendaele Church stood prominent and quite intact on the opposite slope.

In five weeks the Corps Artillery alone had lost (I believe the figure is correct) 568 officers, killed, wounded, or gassed, and other ranks also had lost in proportion. We ourselves had lost one officer (gassed almost as soon as we had got in), five out of our six N.C.O.'s, and twelve gunners or bombardiers. "D" had had a young officer just out from England killed with a sergeant immediately behind our own guns, and a direct hit on one of their dug-outs had deprived them of three more sergeants and two gunners at one fell swoop. The toll had mounted up steadily, and though the C.-in-C. had issued a special appreciation of the bearing of the artillery in these difficult circumstances, we had day by day been feeling more the heavy strain.

Then had come the last days of July. All the conceivable practice barrages had been fired and the Huns made wise to the uttermost.

Then again—amidst rumours that the French were two days late—the storm clouds had gathered from the unfavourable quarter, and finally on the 31st July the great unwieldy barrage had unwound its complicated length in drizzling rain on the Hun lines. The infantry had gone over and reached the "black line" up to scheduled time : but on the "black line" they had lost co-ordination ; when the barrage advanced again they had been late to follow up ; the barrage had rolled on unheeding ; our men, floundering in its wake on hopeless ground and now in a steady downpour, had had to come back and consolidate on the "black line," while the batteries awaited in vain the longed-for order to advance.

. . . .

Well, what was one job more or less after all ? One might as well be hung for a sheep as a lamb, and I should go down to waggon-lines with all the clearer conscience on the 6th, and sleep.... How I would sleep ! I would get down there for lunch if I could, have a

The Battery in action N. of the Menin Road.

The Menin Road.

At the waggon-lines.

quiet ride in the afternoon into "Pop," and come back to waggon-lines for an early dinner and bed. How glorious to wake up once more, and to hear the birds twittering outside! It seemed ages ago since one had done so last, and it was in reality just eight days. My waggon-line billet was in a small farm-house. Madame and her man had been, for those parts, friendly enough. I remembered having tried to convey to Madame that next time I visited her, Ypres would be free. She had not understood, and perhaps it had been just as well.

Yes, a late breakfast, after a sluice-down in the open air, a leisurely toilet, and a stroll round the horses; and then perhaps a real joy-ride, an all-day affair towards Nieppe Forest....

I rang up the battery and gave my orders for signallers and an orderly on the morrow. There was only one other subaltern available for the job, and as the Major was out at the time I deputed myself. It is the unwritten rule.

I read through the standing orders for the Group liaison officers, finished my chapter of *Sonia*—I was to read the next in a very different setting—and went to sleep.

The Menin Road was a populous concern in those days and the varied traffic comforted our gregarious souls as we walked down at a round pace next morning after breakfast to pay our respects *en route* to Infantry Brigade and the senior Artillery Liaison Officer of the Group in the big labyrinth of dug-outs at the bottom of the hill. Hell Fire Corner, though still occasionally shelled "on spec," was no longer the shunned, depressing cross-roads that it used to be. Now it even boasted a military policeman to control the traffic. Ambulance cars and heavy lorries passed and met us. The road was thick with infantry and fatigue-parties of various kinds going up and coming out.

The shattered boughs and fallen branches, which had blocked the unused road before, had now been side-tracked; only dead mules and horses here and there had created fresh obstructions. Fritz was putting most of his metal this morning on to the front line and the ridge where we were due at noon; but even back here he had guns enough to send over his one a minute, searching—now that he might no longer observe—for some of his old favourite spots. So we did not loiter.

At Infantry Brigade they were making their toilet. The senior Liaison Officer told me that battalion had shifted its headquarters during the night: "too hot to stay where it was." He gave me what he understood were the map co-ordinates of their new abode, and I took my departure.

We crossed the old No Man's Land, passed the working-parties at their thankless tasks of road-making in the churned morass, and picked our way warily round the crater lips across the old German front line system till we struck the railway. It did not seem to be getting shelled, and would at least afford better going than if we plunged through the crater-field direct towards the front line. My intention was to nurse the railway for a mile or so, and then, leaving it, to strike across up the ridge in order to hit off "The Rectory," where Battalion H.Q. were reported to be.

I had not been forward myself since the show. It was worse even than I expected. The ground was just beginning to harden in the hot sunshine, but every hole was filled with water and one had to plan out one's course with long detours, jumping precariously from island to island. The rusted wire, half buried in the loose earth, tore one's puttees. The whole place stank. There were very few dead about; the Hun communiqué had probably not lied in saying that their outposts had been lightly held. But the railway embankment gave possible lodgment for the feet and we kept along it as I planned, with six paces between each man and one eye on the 4·2's falling just to our right in the valley. The effect on that ground was only local and we had no fears of splinters.

At last, panting and thirsty, we reached the crest which our infantry were holding. We could see no movement. Over the bleak expanse of shell-holes there was no human being to be seen; one had got to cast one's eye right back to where the working-parties were.

A line of ruined houses and pill-boxes ran along the ridge. One of them was "The Rectory." I went into it; there was a concreted cellar facing Boche-wards, but nobody inside it. I hailed a Red Cross man who was wandering about forlornly. He hadn't seen anyone, didn't know anything.

It was rather annoying. I looked up my book of the rules and tried a cast back to the original map reference for Battalion Headquarters. It must be a ruined pill-box which they were shelling. I waited till there was a pause and then looked inside. No, not a sign of any-one.

Confound Brigade! That part of the programme

must wait, that's all. I had to establish connection by visual with our Brigade signallers at Hell Fire Corner and must plant my lamp.

We went down into one of the pill-boxes on the ridge and deposited the gear. The dug-out was a foot or more deep in water, but must have been a comfortable, secure home. Two wounded infantrymen were lying on the bunks on one side of the dug-out. They told me they had been there since the first day, untended save by chance arrivals. I tried to cheer them up and we offered them our water-bottles.

We stuck the lamp up just behind the pill-box on the top of a bank and flashed it full in the direction of Hell Fire Corner. There was no answer. "Nothing's going right to-day," I thought, and the shells were pitching just to our right and inviting retirement to the safe—if damp—recess beneath us.

But I was overdue and had not found sign or trace of the infantry. The place might be deserted for all the world, save for our little party. I had one more cast round in various ruined pill-boxes on our side of the slope, and then made up my mind to go forward—east —a little. My Major had told me yesterday that our fellows were digging in in front of the ridge. Perhaps the infantry Colonel was with them.

It did not seem very likely, on the forward side of a ridge sloping towards Hunland, but unusual things were done in those days of disorganisation and I had not seen a single infantryman since we left the working-parties behind us early in the morning. Our infantry, if they were not a myth, must be east of me, not west.

I left my signallers still flashing vainly and took my

orderly with me to the forward slope of the ridge. We stalked down a hedge about 50 yards, then turned due right along another. There was another "pill-box" just half right of us.

"That might be them, sir," said my orderly.

We swung sharp right and walked up to it. I saw an unusual helmet. "One of our Tommies decking himself out," I thought. Then another helmet of the same sort, and the truth flashed on me just as it was too late and we were within a few paces of them, with the pill-box between us and home, covered by a couple of German rifles.

A dozen very vivid thoughts raced through my mind. "Somebody's made the most awful howler." "I can't get back." "Where in thunder were our infantry, then?" "This is the end." "I haven't even got a revolver on me." "Prisoner!—what will they say?" "What the devil *will* they say?"

I gave the lad an order and we held up our hands. I will not labour the apology. The back verandah of the pill-box—so it looked—was bristling with amazed and animated Huns. Cut off from retreat, unarmed and utterly flabbergasted, what would you? I stammered out a few words in bad French to their officer and then asked leave to sit down. I was exhausted and quite overwhelmed. So this was the result of my fourteen months of cumulative experience. What a culmination! To walk over No Man's Land on a bye-day in broad daylight into a German nest! Such a thing had never come into our ken that I could remember. And if it had, I should have been the first to pass uncharitable comment. What hideous irony! I looked

at the boy I had led unwittingly into captivity. What
sort of an officer did *he* think I was now? He would
bless me before it was all over, if all one heard, had
read of, was true. Suddenly one began to see the
prisoner-of-war question in a new light. What was it
like really? And all the time I racked and racked my
brains to think whose fault it was, where the mistake
had lain. I knew the range on the map to "The Rectory," which I had just left, and the range of our S.O.S.
barrage. Three hundred yards to play with. I had
come barely a hundred. Perhaps they hadn't known of
this pill-box. To know, O Lord, if only to know—
and I couldn't[1].

That day seemed an eternity. In the evening I heard
the shells from my own battery come whizzing over.
I was to have observed them, five rounds of battery
fire on the German front line at 5 p.m. Since the push
this had been the only method, except by visual; no
wires had lived a day up till then.

My tie alone proclaimed me as an officer. I had left
my tunic and all my impedimenta, with—fortunately—
my notebooks and important papers, in the pill-box on
the ridge.

The orderly in his rough way was comforting. I felt
sorry for the boy. It wasn't his fault anyway.

One had an early insight into the German character.
This lot were Mecklenburgers and good stuff by the
look of them, but desperately dull and earnest. All

---

[1] I did learn later, at Stralsund Camp in Germany, where I met the
Colonel I was then trying to find. He told me his H.Q. on that day had
been 100 yards *north* of "The Rectory," which they had found too hot to
stay in.

day long they sat in that pill-box—three officers and about twenty men—and jabbered. There wasn't a laugh, there wasn't even the semblance of a smile. They smoked cigars most of the time; when food was brought, they gobbled it down like famished wolves and then turned to jabbering and smoking once more. Occasionally a British plane caused a diversion; they rushed to the verandah and craned their necks at it amidst a babel of maledictions. It would have been funny—if one had been in the heart for it—to see the way these fellows took their war. They were perfectly safe, and knew it, until such time as we should attack again. The pill-box must have been sunk a yard or more beneath the ground, and had five feet or more of concrete on every side. Only the back-blast from a shell pitching in their back verandah—short of a direct hit from a heavy gun —could have done much harm. They were wonderfully well camouflaged.

They gave me something to drink but could not spare any food, and I smoked a cigar or two. When it got dark they sent us down under an escort. We had hardly started when a "strafe" began, so we sat in another pill-box and listened to our own shells falling all round and hitting the place more than once.

Then the bombardment died away and we went on our way—across the swampy Hanebeek, past batteries and groups of infantry in open trenches or yet other pill-boxes; into Company Headquarters, a crowded cellar in a farm, where a brief examination of our guides by a pot-bellied, earnest Hun officer took place; and then away again, on over more open, firmer country, up a long slope by a narrow bridle-path, with our shells still falling at intervals round about and fresh corpses of men and horses showing where our guns had found occasional value from searching tracks whose use had been established. The warning *Draht, Draht* ("ware wire") of our surly N.C.O. guide became rarer, we emerged at length on to a regular road, and after an hour or so's walking we were taken into the roomy and laboriously built and fortified quarters of the Regimental Staff. There more depositions were taken by the bullet-headed Brigade Major, a forbidding-looking, efficient little blackguard, I thought, and a good specimen of their military machine. Cigars were provided for our guides and we were marched out again once more, items of passing interest, no doubt, but as human beings inconsiderable. We would be going towards Moorslede. I was dead tired and faint with hunger, but the cool night air blew fresh upon my forehead. We passed ammunition limbers by the score—great, clumsy things they seemed after our neat Q.F. variety—and now and again a company of infantry coming up to the line at the rapid, business-like half run, half walk, which struck one so strangely after our own infantry's measured pace. They seemed to be in high spirits, and had a cheery word for our guides. From what I saw, the German Flanders army went up cheerfully enough in those days to take its hammering.

And then at last, in the grey dawn and after many questionings of passers-by by our somewhat uncertain guides, Moorslede, and a brief halt in a Headquarters of sorts; then on again on the last stage, beyond shell-fire now and knowing—as every German had enviously said to us who could speak English at all—that " the war was *over for us*." It was their stock phrase, and I believed them with a deep-down feeling somewhere— in spite of all the bitterness—that it was so, and that I should at least, given reasonable luck, see home and friends once more.

Into Roulers we fare in a grinding, shaking motor-bus and take our first impression of black rye bread and *ersatz* coffee.

And here we may be left—in a Belgian occupied town, in a stifling, ill-ventilated room, amidst a motley crew of unwashed, sleepy, but not unfriendly Germans; worn with the fatigue and strain of the last long fifteen hours, and at first—for my part—probing vainly for an explanation of it all ; and then, as the tyranny of the stomach grows more ensconced, settling down to the long, absorbing vigil of waiting on the next full meal.

CHAPTER I

A CAMP IN BEING

A BROAD, level, methodically cultivated plain; a horizon of wooded slopes with, every few degrees or so, the suggestion of winding valleys and watercourses; to the northward, the river Weser, Nature's barrier beyond the wire, flowing between us and freedom, and visible from our upper windows in an occasional gleam of silver against the shadows of the steep further bank; to the west of the town, red-roofed and picturesque with adjoining allotments; on the edge of the allotments a large square walled enclosure containing two very recent architectural abominations, eyesores in the general prospect—to wit, *Kaserne* A and B of the *Offizier Gefangenen Lager*[1] Holzminden, that highly advertised Brunswickian retreat which, on a day in September 1917, flung open its hospitable gates to its first English guests, an advance instalment of about thirty from Karlsruhe. Such—in a paragraph—was Holzminden Camp and its environment.

The new Camp had been freely boomed; the *Lager* "Poldhu" had got hold of it and done wonders with it—that mysterious *Lager* "Poldhu" of Germany in war time, which spoke not through wires or wireless and seemingly lacked all means of transmission, but which percolated, none the less, from *Lager* to *Lager* in some mysterious way, so that what should by rights

[1] Officer prisoners-of-war camp.

have remained a close secret in the *Kommandantur*[1] at X in Baden was known all over the Camp at Y in Silesia within a week or so. Thus it was noised abroad in a dozen camps that four had got out from Freiberg and were still at large, that a tunnel scheme had been discovered at the last moment at Magdeburg, and that poor old C—had got "jug" again for hitting a sentry in the parcel office at Ströhen.

Holzminden—so ran the "Poldhu"—was to be the real thing, a prisoner's Mecca—fine, brand-new buildings, spacious grounds, good scenery, good air. The report was discussed and swallowed or pooh-poohed according to temperament. The Schwarmstedt crowd took the news of their impending departure thither with a pronounced sniff. They were—had been for several months —in the Xth Army Corps Area. Holzminden also was in the Xth Army Corps. There could no good thing come out of the Xth Army Corps. Schwarmstedt was in fact sufficiently sceptical of the Xth Army Corps to have remained gladly in its flea-ridden huts, had it not been that the prospect of a winter on the bog-wastes in those flimsy buildings seemed almost intolerable. That fate was reserved in the actual event for Italians, with the usual leavening of neglected Russians.

Accordingly, an advance party of the 'nineteen-fourteener's' and 'fifteeners' of Schwarmstedt packed up their household gods and suffered themselves to be transported to Holzminden. They were told authoritatively that this was going to be merely a stopping-place on the way to Holland and exchange; so they threw

---

[1] Kommandantur means in a prison camp that part set apart for the German personnel, and includes the Commandant's office.

chests-full of tins at the starving Russians who were remaining behind, left their heavy luggage to follow after them, and arrived only with the clothes they stood up in and a suit-case of tins to last them till they reached the border. The border took most of them three months to reach ; the suit-cases were empty in under a week. It was galling, after having been led to believe that they would be dining at the Hague in a few days, to find that they were to remain prisoners for an indefinite period in a camp in which the feeding arrangements were, to put it mildly, as yet incompletely organised. But they had acted unwisely. Three and a half years of doubt and uncertainty should have taught them better than to travel empty-handed so far from their refilling point, or to rely on exchange until they were actually at the border.

Fortunately, however, they were only the advance guard; the main party from Schwarmstedt had yet to come, and when the nakedness of the land and the bleakness of the immediate exchange prospect was really discovered, the wires were set in motion and injunctions passed to the remainder to save what could yet be saved. Anything edible had long since disappeared down the throats of the Russians and would, in any case, have been difficult to reclaim from our unfortunate Allies. But other things of less immediate value were salved; and the main party from Schwarmstedt pulled out in their turn from the bog camp, resigned at least to a temporary stay in their new abode, and properly equipped with the more essential things. It was a regal transport. There were 200 of them, not to mention their hand-luggage, which assumed vast proportions, since everything that was left behind as heavy luggage stood an even chance of being lost in transit, even if transport exigencies in the Fatherland permitted of it ever being put on board a train.

What an arrival that was—the main body from Schwarmstedt ! We raw 'seventeeners,' fresh up in our ordnance boots and Tommies' tunics from the sorting camps of Heidelberg and Karlsruhe in mild Baden, could hardly credit it. We had what we wore, plus, perhaps, an odd shirt which the Belgian ladies in Courtrai might have given us. Here was an eye-opener —Schwarmstedt Camp come to Holzminden under a camouflage of suit-cases ! We leaned out of the windows of "A" Barrack as they staggered in at the main gate, and the Schwarmstedt advance party hailed their friends as the stream rolled on through the inner gate into the camp grounds, and bawled out amidst the general babel disparaging comment on the new camp and its personnel.

Irish Mick in our room was in great form. "Bury your notes," he sang out, "bury your notes. They sthrip ye mother naked." Every one in three of the incoming cortège had not less on him than 50 marks in German currency notes. (*Strengstens verboten*, of course, and a search on arrival was the accepted thing.) So, taking Mick at his word, they sat them down on the dusty *Spielplatz*, made unobtrusive graves with pocket knives, and dedicated their money to the land. Perhaps they were seen. Perhaps the scratches were in some cases too obvious. At all events the Germans became wise ; and one of their N.C.O.'s going round betimes next morning before the party had been able to see to

their investments unearthed no less than 2000 marks!
The Schwarmstedt party lost the first round.

We have digressed somewhat : but those first few
days at Holzminden were days of digressions, of alarums
and excursions, of administration too chaotic even for
a serious strafe. The best organisation in the world
will not get 500 more or less passive resisters satisfactorily transplanted from one place to another without
considerable difficulty, and the German arrangements at
Holzminden were ludicrously insufficient for their task.
The buildings were there, and that was about all. The
crockery had not arrived ; there were three large boilers
in the German cook-house to cater for the bodily wants
of 500 English officers and 100 Germans ; there were
two or three wretched cooking-stoves for our private
use ; there were about half a dozen British orderlies—
the rest, we were told, were on their way ; the bathroom
had not even been begun ; the parcel room was not yet
open, nor was the canteen ; the German staff were in-
complete, new to the ropes, and totally inefficient. The
Commandant was a kindly old dodderer of about seventy
who left everything in the hands of the Camp Officer ;
and the Camp Officer, as we were to know before very
long and as a good many knew quite well already, was
the most plausible villain and the biggest liar in Germany.
Hauptmann Karl Niemeyer will figure perforce largely
in these pages. Let him be introduced to the reader as
he introduced himself to us on our arrival in the camp.
It was one of his stock 'turns.'

Twenty-five of us had arrived at midnight from
Heidelberg, dead tired and hungry, and had been
greeted in fluent Yank beneath the flaring electric lamp

at the door of the Kommandantur by someone whom at
first sight and sound we took to be rather a genial and
sympathetic person. He told us that he was glad to see
us, that he was always glad to see any Englishman, that
he had been great friends with the English himself before the war, and that he hoped to be so again. But
that in the meanwhile war was war. That we had
better, y'know, write straight away to our friends for
our thickest clothes, y'know. It was very cold here in
winter, y'know—(he did not then add that there was
also very little fuel and that wood was going to cost us
18 marks a pailful). He concluded his speech of welcome on a note of old-world hospitality which made us
think of bedroom candles and a comforting 'night-
cap' :—

"So now, yentlemen, I expect you will be glad to go
to your bedrooms. I will wish you good-night. You
will be searched in the morning."

We crawled upstairs full of hope and were sorted
out into three of the upper rooms reserved for new-
comers. There was nothing to eat and no night lingerie
to slip into; and we were locked in because we had not
been searched.

In the morning we appeared again, empty and un-
shaven, for the search. Our kind mentor of the night
before must have pierced our secret, for almost his first
enquiry was whether we had breakfasted. A menial
was then despatched to bid the cook provide breakfast
for the *Herren* with all despatch, and we solaced our
impatience with unreasoned thoughts of a sizzling
rasher, or at least some *wurst*. Breakfast, when it came,
was one cup each of *ersatz* coffee, and lukewarm at that.

But the genial Karl pretended not to understand our disgust.

It must be admitted that he did not confine his innocent pranks to the newly captured. All was fish that came to his net. The only difference was that he got so little change out of those who knew the ropes. They, for instance, might have guessed what "breakfast" (German 1917 version) meant. Also they knew their rights and how far he—and they—could go, pretty well to the last centimetre. So, be it added, did he. It was one thing for the whole camp to laugh at him on *appel* (roll-call). Laughing and shouting on *appel*—Homeric ripples of merriment or short sharp barks from the entire assembly—were recognised as means of entering effective protest when the Germans began to exceed their prerogatives. But it would be quite another thing to tell Niemeyer to his face to shut up. One officer did this and was promptly marched off to the cells. These two had waged bitter war since Ströhen days and the Englishman had renewed the offensive by openly refusing to shake Niemeyer's hand on arrival at Holzminden. It was natural that the latter should get back on him as soon as the opportunity arrived. Holding, as he did, all the scoring cards, Niemeyer never went out of his way to avoid trouble. On the contrary, he welcomed it. His power to deal with the situation to his own satisfaction only failed when, as sometimes happened, his temper passed completely beyond his control.

Under him, and in charge of Kaserne A, was one Gröner, a saturnine, sallow, heavy-moustachioed fellow, reputed a schoolmaster in civil life, and from all appearances a worthy exponent of Kultur. By the Schwarmstedt lot he was known and loathed, and his stomach bulged temptingly as he stalked on to our *appel.*

And there was Ulrich, who arrived shortly after the opening of the camp and assumed command of B Kaserne and its two hundred and fifty inhabitants. Ulrich had stopped something very recently in the Passchendaele fighting and was generally understood to be "swinging the lead." At all events no brisker or jauntier figure was to be seen most days of the week. But if a General hove in sight, or there was a rumour of further drastic combings-out in the home service cadres, Ulrich forthwith assumed a halt and woe-begone gait. His chest caved in, his left leg lagged behind his right, and he appeared supremely miserable and C3. These seizures were chronic, but were noticed to be of brief duration. For the rest, Ulrich was polite, but a doubtful character. To a privileged few he was communicative and expressed his doubts as to the orthodoxy of the conduct of prison camps in the Xth Army Corps. But his billet depended on his keeping in with the authorities ; he was a border-line case for the front, and he had a wife and numerous children. What would you, or he ?

Let us take the opportunity to introduce the rest of the minor characters. There was a *Feldwebel-Leutnant* called Welman who rejoiced—justly enough—in the sobriquet of the "Jew Boy." He had never been to the front, was reported to be permanently unfit and to get fifty per cent. of the profits of the canteen. At all events he was the officer in charge of the Quartermaster's Department in this Camp, and was credited accordingly with a snug war billet. He was not discourteous, but if unduly harassed by his own superiors, or by a long row of sneeringly critical English, he became excited, and his voice used to sound as if it came out of the bridge of his semitic nose. He spoke vile Berlinese and was generally regarded as a harmless enough little soul with a capacity for business.

There was " Square-eyes," an old farmer Feldwebel who had been promised his discharge months since and loathed his present job. He never made an enemy among the English in the camp and used to speak broken English, beaming through enormous horn spectacles. Unfortunately his reign did not last long. Either his discharge came, or he was regarded by the authorities as too mild for his job. At all events he left us comparatively early.

And there were other gentlemen Feldwebels who construed their duties too humanely for the taste of the authorities and were removed ; and one or two who gained full approbation, and remained to add to the gaiety of things.

What a fate to have the charge of officers in a prison camp ! Theirs was not an enviable lot. If they were too severe, they forfeited all moral control over us. If they were too complaisant, they risked losing their jobs. There was no more difficult fence on which to sit and preserve balance. A few—the more democratic—were doubtless intrigued by the idea of exercising control on the sacred officer class ; on most it weighed as an irreconcileable anomaly.

One little fellow, Mandelbrot, curiously combined respect and authority in his behaviour to us. He was

an incorrigible disciplinarian and never allowed any
liberties. But if he had to address a British officer,
whatever the officer's rank, he would click his heels together and stand to attention.

The first ten days at Holzminden were chaos itself.
Even Niemeyer was unable to exert himself as actively
inimical in the complete disorganisation. He was too
busily engaged in strafing his own staff. Moreover, he
was as yet only Camp Officer. The doddering old
Commandant still reigned and Niemeyer's time was
largely spent in interposing his unwelcome oar into
conversations between the Commandant and an ag-
grieved senior British officer.

The English, moreover, were at sixes and sevens
amongst themselves. It was frankly a struggle for food.
Schwarmstedt, as stated, had brought very few tins.
We from Baden had none. The German commissariat
was of course execrable. There was no "common box"
or relief store of tins and food for new-comers such as
had been instituted in the prosperous days of Crefeld
and Gütersloh, when the odd captives straggled in from
the battle of the Somme and found plenty awaiting
them. Parcels had in many cases been already counter-
manded on the strength of the Holland rumour, in
others they were in process of being diverted from
Schwarmstedt, and this would probably be a matter of
weeks. For the first time since 1914 the old campaigners
were casting about for their next meal. It was a new
experience. The German canteen, of course, had nothing
edible for sale. There was barely fuel enough for our
few stoves ; the baths were not yet open ; the beds
were hard and rocky.

It needed but a brief acquaintanceship with the Xth Corps to be able to put one's finger on the *fons et origo mali*, which went much deeper than the doddering Commandant and his graceless Lieutenant. Everything that was unpleasant in our new surroundings had been hatched, we might be sure, at H.Q. from the brain of von Hänisch, the fox, *General Kommandierende* of the Corps. Now von Hänisch, besides being by nature fox-like, had got a bad hammering from the English on the Somme, and had lost many men, and his field command into the bargain ; and now, with a third or so of the British officer prisoners-of-war in Germany under his amiable tutelage, he was not the man to waste any time in getting back on the country which had been the means of breaking him.

The camp was not ten days old before von Renard took a preliminary prowl round his prize covert to appraise the value of his new hunting grounds ; the magic word went forth "*Inspection.*" The taps were turned on ; the available brooms were brought forth ; the British orderlies—what there were of them—were set on to every conceivable form of fatigue ; the German staff worked overtime, and general electricity pervaded the place. And amidst the general preparations the senior British officer girded up his loins for a battle royal and noted down with his faithful adjutant a long list of complaints....

It is the next day, some time after morning *appel*, which the General has attended and which has passed without incident. The senior British officer, the better to forward his many just claims, has ordered a punctiliously correct parade.

From Room 69 on the second floor of Kaserne A we may get a good view of the interview which, one way or the other, is destined to fashion our existence for the immediate future. The General having made a tour of the Camp is about to pass through the gate into the precincts of the Kommandantur. Our senior officer will apply for an interview. The General will doubtless unbend so far as to go through the form of one.

He is surrounded by his staff, as well as by the old Camp Commandant, with his insufferable Camp Officer, the Paymaster, and the other officers attached to the camp. They are grouped respectfully behind their Chief, very splendid in their best uniforms, and stiff as pokers. Every now and again he turns and addresses a question to one of them, and then the poker back grows even stiffer, and the gloved hand goes up to the peaked cap in salute and stays there till the General is pleased to turn away again. How we used to loathe this German habit. One conceived a frantic longing to tear their hands forcibly away and fasten them down. It seemed so thoroughly Prussian, this habit of talking to their superiors as if they were shading their eyes from the sun! How infinitely better our own brisk method seemed than this long-drawn apotheosis!

The interview is graciously accorded and takes place on the bleak patch of grass graced by the euphemistic title of *Spielplatz* and already worn bare by the trampling to and fro of 500 pairs of feet. Here, against the back wall of the squalid cook-house, across one of the dining room tables (symbol of conference!), ringed in by smug supercilious Huns, and with the eyes of his own countrymen riveted on him from the adjoining barrack, our senior officer joins the issue. It exemplifies the scant attention which has been paid to the spokesman of the British community that the interview should be held in the open air, almost as an afterthought, instead of, as it should properly have been held, in the Kommandantur itself.

The senior British officer has no enviable task, but he has at least the armour of experience and knows how far he may go and to what he is entitled. Years of this sort of thing—ever since First Ypres—have taught him that only too well. There is nothing novel to him in this interview ; only that the nature of the Hun opposite to him partakes of the attributes of the fox rather than of the pig, and that he has if possible a stiffer job in prospect than ever heretofore, and one which he would gladly delegate.

It is no sinecure being senior officer in a bad German prison camp. "The stiffest job I ever took on in my life," a veteran of both the Boer and the European war was heard to say once. "I have never known a position where one weak link in one's own argument, one single individual who is beyond control, will so completely crack one's line of defence."

But of that anon. For the present we will follow Major Wyndham at his uphill task, as the interview begins. He trusts to his own moderate German rather than to an interpreter and speaks direct to the Fox, who listens with eyes askance and a sneer on his face.

The first complaint is the building accommodation. It is at present quite inadequate. There are no public rooms, no library, one solitary cook-house, and no bath-room. When are these going to be allowed, please ?

The General confers. The extra cook-house and the bathroom will be put up as soon as possible. As to the public rooms and the library, there is nothing in the Regulations which prescribes for these. They have been permitted in other camps, but that was a luxury.

"But every German officers' camp in England has at least one public room. It is well known."

"That may be. But England is not Germany. It is war-time, and the English officers must learn to do without luxuries."

"Is it to be understood that this is a 'strafe' camp?"

"It may please the English officers to understand that. It is deserved *allerdings*. Next please." The General glances at his watch.

The next complaint is the size of the exercise ground. It is too small to admit of games being properly played. There is plenty of room if the General will permit the barbed wire fence on the southern side to be moved back 15 yards. It will not encroach on the allotments. And a corner at the south-east end of the camp might also with advantage be put inside the wire.

This is a reasonable proposition. As things are, we can play a half-sized game of hockey on the available ground. One half-sized game of hockey will not go far amongst 550. And there is no necessity for the curtailment. Along the southern side of the ground the inner wire runs parallel to the outer wall, but full 40 yards away from it; immediately under the wall are the allotments of the camp staff. There is a space 20 yards in breadth between the wire and the allotments. Why should we not have this? One can do a lot with 20 yards on a hundred yards' stretch in a prison camp.

But Foxy-face knows only too well where he can hit us on the raw, and is obdurate. "Later, perhaps, we will see, but now impossible. Neither can the gymnasium at the south-eastern end, or any of the ground round it, be included."

Next on the programme comes the conduct of the Camp Officer. Why has Hauptmann Niemeyer, whose behaviour at Ströhen Camp has been already reported to and strongly condemned by the *Kriegsministerium* (War Office), been again placed in a position of responsibility in so large a camp? Has the General been made aware of his previous record?

The senior British officer regrets that he cannot command greater fluency as he makes this point-blank attack. If he succeeds, Niemeyer will have to go. If he fails, it will be war to the knife between the two of them, and he knows it.

But the General has already prejudged the issue and our Major might just as well have saved his powder. Niemeyer has been standing with his hand at the peak of his cap for three minutes gabbling all the time. A clever man can get quite a lot of self-justification into three minutes. He will stay. We can trust him for that...the General beams on his faithful henchman.

The Major sees that it is hopeless, but keeps his temper and carries on. There is one more complaint, and a big one, for it touches honour rather than comfort. It is on the delicate subject of parole.

Now it should be explained that in the Great War captivity meant confinement in the strictest sense of the term, and the roystering days at Verdun in the Napoleonic Wars were not repeated. In those days prisoners on parole kept their private apartments, their carriages, and their mistresses, and racketed, if they wished to—so long as they kept within a reasonable and elastic law—to their heart's content. In the Great War it was the wish, rightly and clearly expressed by Lord Grey, that officers should use the privileges of parole to take walks outside the camp only when they could not get sufficient exercise within it to keep themselves fit. When, therefore, in previous camps the British had availed themselves of this privilege, they had been in the habit, before starting on the walk, of handing in a signed card to the Germans on which it was stated that they undertook not to do two things :—to escape or in any way to facilitate future escape, or to damage German property. The arrangement had proved perfectly satisfactory.

But at Holzminden, when the cards were produced for us to sign, there was a whole charter of other things that we must or might not do when we went out for walks. We were required, for instance, to sign to the effect that we would unhesitatingly obey the orders of the German officer or N.C.O. accompanying us ; this hit at the whole basis of the parole idea. We were asked to append our names underneath a clause which stated that we *knew* that the breaking of our parole was punishable with the death penalty ; this merely insulted our intelligence. We were determined that we would either take walks on parole on the terms of heretofore or not take them at all. This spirit of dogged conservatism when there was so clearly everything to lose and nothing much to gain might seem petty and unreasonable, were it not remembered, firstly, that any attempt to interfere with our parole was in honour bound to be furiously contested, and secondly, that if in the course of business you conceded the German an inch, he was pretty certain shortly to make overtures for an ell.

Such, at any rate, is the opinion of the senior British officer, as he now bluntly demands the *status quo ante* in the matter of parole.

The General laughs and turns to his escort. Who are these British after all who should set themselves up on so high a pedestal ? It is known that their parole was broken at Schwarmstedt, in the spirit, if not actually in the letter. The Major asks for corroborative detail. It is given and denied roundly.

The high and mighty *Stellvertreter Kommandierende General* does not lightly brook flat contradiction in his own domain, and begins to lose his temper. In other words, he begins to shout. The word "Baralong," spat out so that all can hear, floats up to our upper window. He is presumably making some general allegation against the lost British sense of honour. Neither is our Major quite so cool as he was ; " Lusitania " counters " Baralong."

There is no further any attempt at concealment and the Fox bares his teeth in a snarl.

"If every Englishman in this command," he storms, "got his deserts he would be shot." And he stalks away with his staff in a white heat of passion.

The senior British officer sends for his Adjutant and an order goes round the camp that all parole cards will be torn up and no walks will take place until an apology is forthcoming.

The apology took months to come. It took weeks

View from Kaserne B, showing skating rink made in January 1918.

only to report the full circumstances of the case to the British Legation in Holland, thence to the Dutch Minister in Berlin, and finally to the Kriegsministerium itself. And in the meanwhile 500 odd British officers took their sole exercise in the slushy compound, pounding round and round the eternal triangle, forbidden to play games, and longing for the frost which would at least enable them to build a slide.

And on the evening after the General's departure a groan went up from the entire *appel* as the Interpreter announced the fact that the aged Commandant had taken his expected departure and that Hauptmann Niemeyer reigned in his stead.

CHAPTER II

NIEMEYER—AND PINPRICKS

WHAT has been told may serve as a prologue. The curtain at Holzminden did not really go up till Niemeyer came into his own. He became on his accession even more truculent than hitherto. War was openly declared between himself and the senior British officer. The cells rapidly filled up with officers whom he had incarcerated for an innocuous stare, a failure to salute at 30 paces distance, or more than likely for no reason at all. We became accustomed to the sight and sound of this gentle knight outside our Kaserne in the morning about a quarter to eight, storming up and down in a black gust of bilious passion, harrying everybody—Germans, British, officers, orderlies—anyone, in short, who crossed his path. "I give you three days right away," "I guess you know I am the Commandant," and similar phrases floated up to us as we lay in bed half asleep and warned us that we might expect a visit at any moment. Sometimes, in the beginning, he came into our rooms in person and made facetiously offensive remarks to our unresponsive forms. But later his sense of dignity deprived us of the pleasure of his company at these early hours, and he preferred to prowl about outside in general supervision, while sentries and N.C.O.'s, acting to orders, and sheepish or blatant according to their natures, banged upon our doors, and with a raucous *Aufstehen* ("get up") contrived as a rule to bring back reality.

We were supposed to be up by 8 o'clock. If we were not, there was always the risk that one of the sentries might interpret his duties too literally and pull us out. This insult was of quite frequent occurrence, and it resulted, as may be supposed, in friction of the most serious kind. Someone would probably shout down at Niemeyer in the enclosure "Take your — sentries away," and Niemeyer would at once storm his way up to have a personal investigation on the spot. The hate at that unseasonable time in the morning could be very direct, and usually resulted in the Commandant bagging a brace or so more for "jug."

It need not be added that these visits aroused intense resentment. It was so obvious that they were only intended to annoy. The pretext was that we were so habitually late on the 9 o'clock *appel*. The answer to that was that in a crowd of 500 odd a great many would be late at any *appel*, be it fixed for 9 or 10, or even 12. Let those who were late take their chance of punishment. Another argument advanced by Niemeyer was that according to the regulations every room had to be swept and garnished by 10 A.M. Our reply was that they always were. Our own orderlies were responsible for that job, and they performed it when they were not called away from their own task on a German fatigue. And in their unavoidable absence we cleaned up our rooms and made our beds ourselves.

This little game was in fact no more than one of a series of pinpricks ; taken by itself we could have made light of it. But the snowball of pinpricks gathered weight as the camp got under weigh and Niemeyer grew more and more secure in his position.

Niemeyer succeeded in impregnating the entire camp with an atmosphere of acute discontent and jumpiness, and no one knew this better than himself. It was, as a matter of fact, a remarkably fine achievement for one man, for Holzminden might have been from the start a happy camp. The air was good, the view was good, the buildings were waterproof, the water supply was good. Only the Commandant was vile.

The man who controlled the welfare of approximately one-quarter of the English officers at this time prisoners-of-war in Germany had for 17 years besmirched by his presence the province of Milwaukee, U.S.A. His twin brother, Heinrich, of Clausthal Camp in the same command, boasted a similar record—what they had done during the 17 years nobody exactly knew. The brethren were practically doubles, and rivalled each other in the calculated arrogance, animosity, and deceit which, for the best part of a year, busied a thousand souls in devising suitable post-bellum punishments for the estimable pair. If a comparison had to be made, it might be said by those in a position to know that Harry was the worse on occasions, but that Charlie had it for sheer, dogged, day-in day-out nastiness. In any case there was not much in it.

It was a concatenation of unfortunate circumstances that two watch-dogs of such a breed and temper happened to be lying idle in the Hanover kennels when the word went forth for a general British strafe in the Xth Army Corps. It was always understood that the pair had weathered a search on the high seas by a British destroyer when crossing over from America to the service of their beloved Fatherland. As to Charles, it was reported that he had been given some form of a command on the Somme, but had lost it again within a brief period. He was certainly fond of referring in no uncertain way to his dreadful experiences in that battle—which was, if anything, a pretty sure indication that he had never been near it.

The reason for the high favour in which the Niemeyers were held at Hanover was always something of an enigma. It was supposed by some that they could trace their patronage to even Higher Quarters than the Army Corps Commander. The appointments of Camp Commandants, we were once told by a friendly Dutchman from the Berlin Legation, were in the giving of the Emperor. He alone could make and unmake. There was no reason to suppose this particular Dutchman was lying to us, and he had come straight from the Hague, where Lord Newton was at the time endeavouring to thrash out an acceptable exchange agreement with the German representatives. Certain it is that, despite the strongest representations ever since the departure of the first party for exchange to Holland—from British officers to the British General commanding in that country, from the General to the War Office, from the War Office back again to the British Legation in Holland, from the Legation to the Dutch Government, and from the Dutch Government to Berlin—the pair stuck like leeches, and retired, by the back door, only at such an advanced period in the war that it had become evident that not even the patronage of the All Highest was likely to avail them much any longer. If true, it is an index of the system.

But most of us were sceptical of this explanation. It appeared more reasonable to suppose that the Niemeyers were helping Hänisch in butter from our parcels and getting carte blanche as a *quid pro quo*. There is no doubt at all that Charles used to steal, although he took good care to cover his tracks[1].

In appearance they were typically Hunnish, but of the commercial rather than the military brand. Bullet heads with close-cropped grey hair; florid complexion; grey moustachios with the usual Kaiser twirl; heavy jowl and thick neck. Charles Niemeyer used to wear his cap at a rakish angle on the back of his head. He was never seen out of his Prussian military greatcoat except during a severe heat wave, or without his spurs. Like most of his countrymen he carried a swelling paunch, which protruded as he walked or stood even more prominently than its circumference warranted. Sometimes he carried a stick, but more usually he thrust both hands deep into his greatcoat pockets, from which they were only occasionally withdrawn to return a salute. He smoked large numbers of cigars. All these outward characteristics gave him a most plebeian appearance singularly at variance with that of the usual dapper and punctilious regimental officer.

His voice was the most astounding thing about him. It was really a most delicately modulated instrument capable of the softest and most sycophantic coo or the most guttural bellow, as occasion demanded. Niemeyer used to speak his native tongue extremely fast, babbling along without any of the harsh scraping dissonances that one usually associated with it, and quite unintelligibly

---

[1] When the parcel room at Holzminden was cleared out after the armistice, a trap-door was found in the floor, thus allowing access from under the guard-room. Niemeyer expressed the greatest astonishment.

Karl Niemeyer.

to the ordinary English ear. His English was simply
bar-tender Yank, extremely fluent within certain stock
limits and every now and then including a ludicrous error;
also, when he wished it, suitably foul. He sometimes
made absurd mistakes. Thus he would say "I will have
you arrested right now—in five minutes," or (his best)
"You think I do not understand the English, but I
do. I know dam all about you."

"Right away," "cost price," the enclitic "Yes-no" at
the end of a sentence, and other absurdities abounded
in his speech. "Cost price" was a particular favourite.
You could get "cost price" jug for any period : or you
could be "told something straight, yes cost price, I guess."
He cherished the idea that "cost price" represented what
was plain and unequivocal, an index to the straight-dealing
methods of alien saloon managers in far Milwaukee.
Sometimes, when a grievance involved the use of technical
English beyond his range, he would blind at us in German,
which we infinitely preferred, as it gave the comedians
an opportunity for looking uncomprehendingly asinine
and shouting in chorus *nichts verstehen* ("don't understand"), which infuriated him.

With Niemeyer first impressions were not actually
unpleasing, as he had clear blue eyes and a voice which,
as I have said, when under control was not unmusical.
New arrivals at the camp, unless they had been forewarned or had had previous dealings with him, were inclined to size him up as a friendly, if over-familiar, old
bounder.

He used to walk about with a retriever puppy, which
was a source of considerable annoyance to its owner, as
it was invariably on better terms with the prisoners-of-

war, who used sometimes to feed it, than with himself. The only occasions on which he was ever seen to stoop was when bending down to coax the puppy to follow its rightful master.

He treated his dependants as beings of another world —"like dogs" would be too mild a term, for Niemeyer was quite restrained in his dealings with the puppy. He was never seen to return his men's salutes; he only returned ours as the result of frequent protests. His conduct towards the British orderlies was just the same, except that his vituperation had to be done in English and with therefore more limited scope. To the British officers, except in his moods of Berserker fury, he would be either coldly polite or else offensively hail-fellow-well-met, as the mood took him. If he had any hobbies we did not hear of them. He neither walked nor rode nor indulged in any sport. Once in a blue moon he went for a drive. He was a bachelor, and was understood to loathe the sight of women. Whether he drank or drugged or gambled his many spare hours away at Holzminden is not known. We did not certainly identify him with literary tasks. The knowledge of his power was his main solace, and there is no doubt that he often stirred up trouble in the camp for the sake of trouble. To some such motive only could be ascribed his relentlessly literal interpretation of the Corps regulations. Under a reasonable régime these would never have been pressed. Even so, things at Holzminden would have gone smoothly enough if he had been a gentleman. It was the fact that even this modest provision had not been made on their account that goaded the British to an intense intolerance of the man and all his works; and he, in his turn, looked for moral support to the authority which, with full knowledge, had placed him where he was. Such was Captain of the Reserve Karl Niemeyer.

He adopted the policy of alleviating our numerous discomforts only by slow degrees or on the principle of two steps backward for each one forward. A long string of complaints was presented to him on the average about twice a week. The bath-house was at length completed, and the camp watch-dog was promptly lodged in it. When remonstrated with, Niemeyer explained that there was at present no room for the dog's accommodation in the Kommandantur. So we continued bath-less for another month—those of us, at least, who could not face an icy plunge in the horse-troughs on the *Spielplatz*. When at length the bath-house was vacated and purged, it was found that only two of the showers were effective.

Somebody broke one of the electric lamps in the compound : all games were promptly stopped. This left us literally with no outlet for exercise except the monotonous "pound" in shorts and jersey round the camp enclosure, or a furtive game of fives at the end of one of the long corridors, for which it was not always easy to "book a court"!

The distribution of parcels was kept in the hands of the German personnel, and as a result hopeless chaos and congestion reigned. In all previous camps the British had efficiently organised the distribution of their own parcels, no light task in the days when supplies from home were unrationed and one recipient might claim as many as twenty parcels in a week. When the consignments diverted from other camps began to reach Holzminden, the German parcel room was packed from floor

to ceiling with the accumulations. The most that Niemeyer would at first allow in the nature of English
control in the parcel room was the services of two
orderlies. The presence of a British officer in the parcel
room, even on parole and for the express purpose of
supervising and facilitating delivery, was only permitted
when all other attempts to cope with the situation had
failed.

It was the same with the tin rooms, and here a word
of explanation is required. When a prisoner-of-war in
Germany drew his parcel from home he might not,
strictly speaking, merely walk off with it under his arm.
This practice was winked at in many easy camps, but
at Holzminden it was rigidly taboo. The regulations
stipulated that every article should be strictly censored
before issue. It was not enough to shake a tin to
ascertain its non-contraband nature. It had to be opened
by a German and its contents taken delivery of in a
plate or bowl. And if the contents were solid, such as,
for instance, a tinned ham, then that ham had to be cut,
bisected, quartered, or "Crippened" into just so many
fragments as would leave no room for doubt that a
compass or a map or a file did not remain concealed.
A ham or tongue, of course, was thus ruined. The
German employees in the tin room loathed this desecra-
tion almost as much as we did ; it gave them additional
work and seemed to them to be an act of unreasoning
vandalism. Poor devils! Some of them were honest,
although undoubtedly some stole. But it must have
been refined torture for them daily to sniff Elysium and
lack its joy, daily to mutilate *delicatessen* such as they
had not tasted for months and months, daily to handle

forbidden delights. But they had to do it, for they never knew when the Commandant would not spring a surprise visit on them. I have seen him take out a penknife on such occasions and hack practically into mincemeat a tongue which had been left comparatively whole, full of zest for the service of the Fatherland and threatening dire things to his staff if ever such an object was let off so lightly again.

But even the destruction of our food would have been tolerable if we could have got at it with reasonable ease; unfortunately the inadequacy of the arrangements extended to the cellars where the tin rooms were located. At the beginning of things there was one tin room for the requirements of the whole camp. The tins were brought down from the parcel room in wheelbarrows and piled on racks in the tin room; there was no British supervision; there were no lockers or partitions, and the German staff could not read or understand English. It was hardly to be wondered at, therefore, that before a week was out the room was in complete confusion, accentuated each day as the intake exceeded the offtake.

To get your tins opened you had to take your turn in a queue. To be the first man in this queue it was necessary, as a rule, to put in an appearance about half-past seven in the morning. The last applicant was usually served just before evening roll-call. All day the queue crawled. It was a case of queue-crawling or missing a day, English tins or German rations, and the inner man won. The head of the queue was at the tin room door. The rest of it coiled along the damp passage which traversed the cellar floor, it sat and read on the steps of the staircase that led down to the passage, often it over.

flowed right into and out of the doorway of the Kaserne. It was a mournful dispirited queue in those days. The Germans took five or ten minutes to serve each man and it was even odds that your tins wouldn't be there[1]. And if you were very unlucky you might have an accident with your tray on the return journey, upset your plates, and have to begin all over again.

So much for tins; but even so, the toil was not complete. Supposing that you had emerged, weary but victorious, from the cellars, you had still only the cold and raw material for your meal; the urgent corollary was to get this cooked, and to do so it was necessary to fight for a place on the stoves. Holzminden at that time boasted three cooking stoves with surface space for thirty pots (including kettles) and a purely wood fuel supply. It was hardly to be wondered at—so great was the demand, and so slow the fire—that a great many did not get on the stoves more than once in the day. It is true that new and better stoves were being built opposite to B Kaserne, but they were not yet ready. For the moment it was a case of opportunism, watchfulness, forcefulness if necessary, and devil take the hindmost.

Sometimes the old German cook would take part of the overflow on to his own capacious stoves in the German cook-house and so ease the congestion. But he was in deadly terror all the time that he would be seen helping us from the Kommandantur, and he expected a

[1] Practically everything in an English parcel was tinned. An officer's visit to the parcel room showed him what he ought in due course to get when his tins had passed the censorship of the tin room. Between the two rooms was considerable leakage.

substantial consideration (in kind) for the risk he took on our behalf. Such consideration it was not in the power of some of us to bestow.

We from the sorting camps were feeling the pinch about now, and were living, most of us, and apart from the German ration, on precarious charity. At Karlsruhe we had blown ourselves out on tomatoes and bread : at Heidelberg we had added relish to the bread with an occasional pot of honey from their well-stocked canteen. But in the canteen at Holzminden there was nothing to eat beyond a very nauseous paste. Some of us were lucky and fell in with a well-stocked mess ; the rest of us waited blankly for our relief parcels, eking out with a tin here and a tin there, frying bread in dripping, lucky if we could see a meal ahead. For the first time in our lives we knew hunger ; not so fiercely as our successors in 1918 were to know it, but more fiercely perhaps than the veterans of 1914 and 1915, who, whatever their other tortures, had at least come as prisoners into a country where food was to be had for the purchasing.

Finally there was the question of fuel. It was October now, and the days in Brunswick were no longer balmy. Each of our rooms—scheduled to hold twelve—possessed a stove, but there was nothing to put in the stove. We saw woods on the horizon to three sides of us. The regulations, we understood, permitted us the daily ration of a German soldier in the field. But no wood was forthcoming, except what was brought for the consumption of our three cooking stoves. A dangerous minority endeavoured, as usual, to destroy the comfort of the community by stealing this cooking supply. The practice was sternly stopped. Then recourse was had to the stools in the dining rooms. These blazed well for a night or two, but were naturally not replaced, and we had all the fewer stools to sit upon. Finally those who preferred a blaze to a night's rest sacrificed their bed boards. It was reckless jettison, but excusable. The Camp Commandant had broken faith with us over the fuel question, if possible more flagrantly than over others, and the camp was justly incensed. One day a representative of the Dutch Legation in Berlin had been down to visit us. On the morning of his arrival the Commandant, scenting the trouble which might be expected on this as on other issues, had caused it to be proclaimed at morning *appel* that from that day fuel would be issued free (loud cheers!). We might have known. We never got a faggot free. The representative carried out his colourless inspection, and that evening we were as cold as before. The end of this particular campaign was that ultimately, and under the extreme pressure of the increasing cold, we paid for wood at the rate of 40 marks a cubic metre. The only people who got fuel free were those under detention in the cells.

Every now and again a waggon-load of briquettes used to come in under escort for discharge in the coal cellars of Kaserne B. On these occasions we used to help unloading the waggon—but not into the coal cellars. A crowd of officers with British warms and trench coats with capacious pockets suddenly appeared from nowhere, swarmed round the waggon and its disconcerted sentinel, and contrived to get a bit of their own back.

For rank exploitation, however, the food supply was *facile princeps*. We might forgive the Germans for the food they offered us; we could not forgive them either

for the way they served it or for the price they made
us pay for it.

In one of the cellars aforementioned our year's potato
supply was stored. This came in in October. Three
English orderlies were on permanent fatigue in this cellar,
peeling the daily potato ration for the camp. When the
peeling was complete the potatoes were thrown into one
of the two large coppers in the German cook-house (the
other contained hot water) and were boiled up in re-
lentless conjunction with the other ingredients billed for
that particular day. It did not matter what they were;
everything went into the hotch-potch, and, so long as it
eventually boiled and was ladled out into big pails for
despatch to the dining rooms, all was well. On Sundays
there was an occasional lump of horse-flesh floating in
the stew and some green vegetable which might fairly
be classified as "a not too French French bean"; on
one Sunday, as a variation, the skull of a cow complete
except for skin and ears was found floating in the pot.
On other days plain *sauerkraut*, or its equivalent nastiness.
Occasionally there was some barley grain which, with
many of us, did duty as porridge for our next morning's
breakfast.

Such was our bill of fare for the mid-day meal. Our
breakfast was *ersatz* coffee : our supper was an attenuated
version of our lunch. And for this we were mulcted
monthly to the tune of 60 marks a head. No doubt this
charge would have been exceeded, if it had been possible ;
but an agreement between the British and German
Governments had fixed the sum of 60 marks as the limit
which a subaltern prisoner-of-war might receive as pay
whilst in captivity, and the Germans could not therefore

legally charge any more. As it was, there was nothing left on which a subaltern might come and go for ordinary out-of-pocket expenses in the canteen or in camp subscriptions; and to meet these requirements he had to draw a cheque on his bankers which was discounted with a neutral agent by the Germans at a ruinous rate of exchange for himself and with a very comfortable margin of profit for everybody else concerned.

No one, of course, who could live on his own supply of tins thought of looking at the German food. It was too impossibly served. Messes would sometimes depute one of their members to make a dive into the soup tub and rescue some of the better looking potatoes wherewith to supplement the evening stew.

The poor quality of the diet was accepted as directly attributable to the beleaguered state of Germany. We knew that the sentries and the staff personnel were getting the same, and that probably the people in the town were faring little better. What we did resent was that we were not allowed to take over our ration in bulk and exercise control as to the manner of its cooking, and also that we were not allowed a rebate for what we did not require.

There was only one visible means of retaliation—scrupulously "drawing" the whole of the weekly ration of Boche bread and as scrupulously wasting it or burning it. That never failed to create a commotion, and it was made, before very long, a punishable offence.

Almost weekly the messing question figured prominently on the agenda for the senior officer's conference with the Commandant. Weekly the same privileges were demanded—control of the raw supply, supervision in the kitchen, an equivalent return in money for what we did not require. Weekly the Commandant returned evasive and unsatisfactory replies, and shifted the onus of responsibility on to convenient and distant Hanover. To the end we were not quite sure that he might not, in this one instance, be really telling the truth. The messing system in the Hanover command might really conceivably be directed from a centralised control; but if so, how to reconcile our system with that at Clausthal in the same command, where rebate was allowed as a matter of course?

Later on, damning evidence was collected to prove that we were not getting more than two-thirds of our scheduled weight. As a sop we received the unheard-of concession of getting our potatoes in their jackets on two days in the week.

There is little doubt, in the retrospect, that our messing at Holzminden probably afforded the easiest field for exploitation, so little interest was taken, during most of the period, in the garbage which was offered us, and so regular and secure was the payment, a credit from our own unsuspecting Government debited automatically against us in our account before we had even the opportunity to turn it into *Lager Geld*, as the paper currency of the camp used to be called. It was hardly to be wondered at that the Supply branch of the German army should have been so venal; the opportunities for profiteering must have been unlimited.

Sometimes a Quartermaster-General used to come round on inspection and sniff the mess in the coppers and admire the stoves. With him in close attendance one probably saw the people who were really getting at us, the *Verwaltung Leute* ("Q" people) of the place. They were seedy, suspicious-looking folk, thin enough in spite of their obvious battening at our expense. The General himself was a fairly poor specimen of his class. He drove up to the camp from the station even in the finest weather in a closed carriage and behind one feeble nag. He was obviously zealously misinformed about everything, and our quarrel lay not with him, any more than we should have visited the sins of an over-astute quartermaster on the shoulders of some old dug-out at Corps H.Q.

Later on, in 1918, we heard how things had been done at Rastatt in Baden, where hundreds of British officers lay all day on their beds too weak to move for weeks on end. There too, where the stuff that we spurned would have been a banquet, the fault could be brought home to the criminal maladministration, venality, and neglect of the ghouls on the lower rungs of the *verwaltung* staff. We have seen the diaries—

"Thursday half ration, complained but no explanation. Friday a General came over to inspect. We were given a double ration for dinner. Saturday half ration again": and so on.

But in their case it was deliberate cruelty as well as exploitation.

CHAPTER III

INTRODUCING THE MAIN MOTIF

SUCH, in brief, were some of the major pinpricks in this winter of our discontent. Needless to say that from the beginning heads had been put together to discover a means of escape. The camp did not, at first sight, appear an easy one to get out of, but before we had been there a month seventeen had been out. A hole was made in the passage of Kaserne A at the end next to the Kommandantur and through this parties in twos and threes, and even in sixes and sevens, had crept, walked down the stairs of the Kommandantur and, in the guise of German sentries under an N.C.O., made their exit through the main gate. When the first party got away—three of them—their names were answered for them on *appel* for the next day and a half, giving them two full days' start. This was the more creditable performance as one of them was a field officer, and as such paraded on *appel* with the few other officers of his rank in the camp in front of the vulgar herd, easy to be seen and equally easy to be missed.

Unfortunately Niemeyer's luck was in. All were caught before they reached the Ems and were brought back to the camp. The passage was discovered, the hole was filled up, a system of permit cards initiated, and the most promising escape channel in the camp was abandoned as being no longer practicable. Niemeyer was immensely relieved when the last of his errant lambs was brought back for incarceration. He had had his lesson and profited by it. Henceforth the English should be allowed no rope.

So the wire was heightened and a No Man's Land was created round the enclosure between the line of sentries and the Platz, wherein it was death to walk. Censoring redoubled in vigilance. British control in the parcel room seemed more distant an event than ever, and Niemeyer became more blatantly cocksure than before.

"You see, yentleman," he would, say, "you cannot get out now. I should not try ; it will be bad for your health."

And in reply, and having nothing very much better to do, a select little band assumed the habits and characteristics of moles and started on the long task which was to result in convincing Niemeyer that he had made a mistake, and that where there is a will there is also somehow and somewhere a way.

The history of the Holzminden Tunnel is the history of a great adventure. It was over 60 yards in length, and it took nine months to complete. It was dug, except for one brief period, in the hours of daylight between morning and evening *appel*, and its workers, in order to reach and return from the scene of their labours, ran daily risks of being identified by the German sentries. Much of it was dug through layers of stones ; all of it was dug with appliances that a miner would have scorned. During all its long travail it was never actually suspected—and this though the Camp Commandant prided himself as the "cutest" gaoler in the Fatherland. Lastly, it was above all expectations successful, and in a way which satisfied to the full the dramatic proprieties.

An attempt has been made in this story to show its readers something of Holzminden Camp as it was, not because it bristled with barbarities, as some previous accounts of it might have led credulous people to believe, but because it did most effectively supply a suitable background to the tunnel episode; a background of grey, monotonous imprisonment, of minor indignities considerable only in their cumulative effect, of permanent tension, of seeming unendingness, and a queer depression beyond the ordinary. All who were there will testify to that. Holzminden, even in its lighter moments, was a gloomier camp than many where the actual conditions were infinitely worse.

The secrets of the tunnel are not the author's at first hand; he did not personally experience its dark embrace; he did not "labour and pray" in its recesses with a sense of intimate proprietorship. In fact, except for some organising assistance on the actual night of the escape, he had nothing actively to do with it. The control of the enterprise rested in the hands of a select few who were known as the "working-party" and on whom devolved the whole responsibility of doing the job and seeing that it was done in secret. It was impossible for those whose business it was to keep in close personal touch with the whole community to remain long in ignorance of the identity of the various members of this party. But what they were doing, how or exactly where they were doing it, when they would finish doing it—on these points one was not, and did not expect to be, enlightened. When the working-party discussed plans, they did so behind closed doors and in an undertone. The results of their deliberations were communicated to those whom it concerned and to those alone. Once the shifts had been arranged there was no need for a member of the party to do more than be in his appointed place at the appointed time and carry out his appointed task. In the intervals the less he talked the better. It was only when the scheme was nearing its maturity and when it became desirable to let a favoured few into the secret that tongues began ever so circumspectly to wag.

When the essay became an event, and the tunnel the one topic of conversation through the camp—and, be it said, through Hanover as well—it was possible to join the odd ends together and follow the whole enterprise through in the retrospect from its modest beginning to its glorious conclusion. This is all that this account pretends to do.

At this juncture it may be well to describe the premises.

The two Kasernes were identical in structure, but the fact that the near end of Kaserne A was sacred to the Kommandantur and the far end of Kaserne B was set apart for orderlies gave rise to some more or less improvised alterations in the internal structure. Here it should be mentioned that "near end" means nearest to the main gate. As you walked in through the main gate the Kommandantur lay immediately on your left, the sentries off duty sniggered at you from the guard-room on your right, and the officers' enclosure through another (inner) gate directly faced you. The portion of Kaserne A set apart for the English was that part which was beyond the inner gate. The windows of the nearest

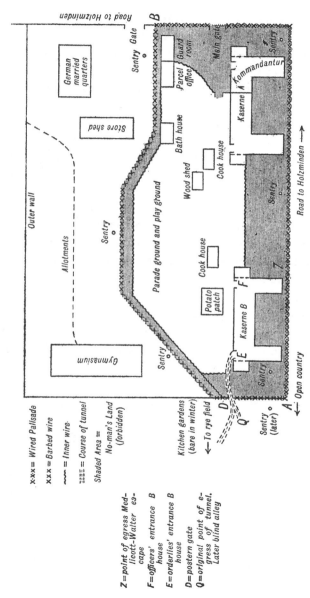

General plan of Holzminden Camp

(Scale approx. 1 inch = 50 yards)

xxx = Wired Palisade

xxx = Barbed wire

~~~ = Inner wire.

==== = Course of tunnel

Shaded Area =
No-man's Land
(forbidden)

Z = point of egress Med-
licott-Walter es-
cape

F = officers' entrance B
house

E = orderlies' entrance B
house

D = postern gate

Q = original point of e-
gress of tunnel.
Later blind alley

room to the gate on the ground floor were whitewashed
in order that we might not read—and thereby be in a
position to copy—the permit cards which it was necessary for every German, military or civilian, to show the
sentry on duty before being permitted to pass in or out
of the prisoners' enclosure. This regulation was a safe-
guard introduced after the original escapes, and it used
to afford some amusement. On one occasion a sentry,
having been duly cautioned as to his orders, let Niemeyer himself through without asking him for his card.
The result was an intensification of the air in the neigh-
bourhood for a good five minutes, and loud sounds
of merriment from the British quarter. Next day the
fellow, on his metal, stopped Niemeyer—in a hurry. The
sentry said very little, Niemeyer said a very great deal;
the consequence was that the sentry got seven days for
his pains, and the world—meaning the British quarter—
again cooed with merriment. But that is by the way.

Going straight on down the main cobble-stoned
thoroughfare of the camp, you reach Kaserne B, about
70 yards apart from Kaserne A.

Kaserne B was a 50-yard long, ugly, four-storied
affair, with an entrance doorway and a flight of stairs at
each end of it. From each entrance doorway a few steps
downward brought you through another door to the
basement corridor—(the distinction between these doors
should be kept clear in mind). On the outer side of
this basement corridor, i.e. looking towards the uncommunicative outer wire of the camp, were the punishment cells; on the inner side were the various cellars—
the tin cellar, the bread cellar, the store cellar, and potato
cellar, and other cellars necessary for the economic

Kaserne B.

administration of the camp. Half way down the basement corridor, and shutting off the British from any
possibility of prying into the cellars at its far end, was
a partition consisting of two doors usually locked.

The near entrance door was the officers' entrance, the
far door the orderlies' entrance. Going through a swing
door *opposite* the officers' entrance on the ground floor,
you found yourself in a long corridor which traversed
the entire length of the building and connected about a
dozen large rooms wherein the inhabitants of the ground
floor lived, slept, and made shift generally. The rooms
averaged about twelve occupants apiece and looked out
on to the inner (enclosure) side. The lower part of
their windows had to be kept permanently shut, even
in the daytime, a source of never-failing contention and
resentment.

The first floor was the counterpart of the ground
floor, except that the windows might be opened and
the general appearance was correspondingly brighter.
At the end of each of these floors were the "small"
rooms which opened off in little passages or saps at
either end of the main corridor. These small rooms
constituted the wings of the main building, which was
constructed after the pattern and in the proportions of
an E minus its central appendage. The sketch shows
this clearly enough.

These rooms were keenly competed for. They held
three to four occupants each and the actual amount of
cubic space per occupant was less in them, if anything,
than in the larger ones. But the moral effect of only
having to reckon with the individual proclivities of two,
as against eleven other of your fellow-men, was reck-

oned as an inestimable advantage; and no sooner was the rumour abroad of one of those periodical "general posts" occasioned by the departure of a party for exchange to Holland or elsewhere than the House Adjutant's[1] room was besieged by a crowd of applicants and their backers, the insistence of whose claims was, as a rule, in exactly inverse proportion to their merit. Thus A, who is being strongly run for the shortly-to-be-vacant billet in Number 35, is a second lieutenant with eight months' experience of captivity, and B, whose inclusion in Number 37 opposite seems no less essential to its existing occupants, is a Flying Corps captain aged 21, not yet through his first six months of *gefangenschaft*. C and D, however, who have commanded companies on the Somme, remain unchampioned and unambitious in their large rooms amidst a welter of disorder, discomfort, and possibly discord, and have to be prodded into admitting that they wouldn't mind if they *did* get a little peace now and again. It is the way of the world.

On the second floor there was the difference that two large dining rooms were interspaced between the living rooms. Dining room, it should be added, was a term purely of courtesy. It is true that in these rooms the large majority of officers in the Kaserne stored their cooking utensils, prepared their food for cooking, and gulped it down as quickly as might be when cooked. But this feature of the rooms was not stressed, and they were used in turn, and during the greater part of

---

[1] At Holzminden the senior British officer worked through a personal adjutant, known as the Camp Adjutant, who handed on orders to officers in charge of each Kaserne, known as House Adjutants.

the day, as theatres, lecture rooms, concert rooms, reading rooms, and churches; on Saturday nights, or whenever a "show" was on, officers were requested to have finished their dinner by six. Dinner over, the cups and plates were dumped in a convenient corner, the tables were pushed up together to one end of the room to form a solid platform, and in an incredibly short space of time the drop scene and the wings were hoisted triumphantly. Then, after two hours' rapt forgetfulness of the surroundings, down came the final curtain, out trooped the audience, and back the tables were pushed into their respective sites. The drill was clockwork. There was nothing that we would less willingly have foregone than our "shows," and the scene-shifters would have done so least of all.

But we must leave the dining rooms and mount the stone staircase once again to the attic floor. This consisted of a few small rooms at the near (Kommandantur) end, and the orderlies' quarters, with a stout wooden partition, strengthened with sheet iron, in between. The small rooms were remarkable only for their extreme cold and the fact that one of them played a highly important part in the subsequent proceedings. The orderlies occupied the farther end of the attic floor. We had the opportunity of inspecting their quarters when we went up at certain fixed times to the baggage room, which was at that end of the passage, to remove, under the surveillance of a German Feldwebel, such articles as we might require from our heavy luggage. To do so we of course used the further (orderlies') staircase. This was supposed to be the only occasion on which the officers might enter the building by the further doorway. To check irregularities in this respect a sentry was always placed at a spot outside the outer wire and exactly opposite the doorway.

It should be added that—as the barrack was originally built—the far ends of the ground, first, and second floor corridors were exact replicas of the near ends, and gave directly on to the orderlies' staircase through swing doors. These doors had at the outset been securely boarded up. Early in the history of the camp a trap-door had been made by some officers through the boards on the dining room floor, but it had been discovered by the Germans, who were now on their guard for any repetition of the attempt; so that it was now a physical impossibility to reach the orderlies' quarters or their staircase by any other means than walking in at the further doorway. Similarly, orderlies could not reach their own quarters except through their own door.

From the near door of Kaserne A (the Kommandantur door) to the far (orderlies') door of Kaserne B was a distance of some 150 or 160 yards and constituted the base of the segment formed by the conformation of the buildings and enclosure. The arc of the segment was represented by the barbed wire fence with its neutral zone which ran from just opposite the orderlies' door (E)—where it joined the outer wall—round the semi-circular *Spielplatz* till it merged in the parcel room and guard room opposite the Kommandantur. The space thus enclosed between the base of the segment and the arc represented the gross amount of outdoor elbow room for the inmates of the camp, and measured about 410 yards round. The net available space was much less. One German and two English cook-houses, a twenty-yard square potato patch, a wood shed, cobble-stones, horse troughs, parallel bars, and a cinder path running inside the wire, were factors which considerably reduced our field of sport.

Just behind the length of the two Kasernes ran the outer barrier, barbed wire superimposed on iron palings five or six inches apart, with sentries on the inside and later on the outside beat as well. The whole of the ground directly between the two Kasernes, and again between them and the outer barrier, was No Man's Land and forbidden to the British.

If you looked from the whitewashed window at the end of the ground floor corridor in Kaserne B, you saw an eight-foot wall between you and freedom. This wall ran at right angles from the far end of the wired palings and was wired on top. There was a sentry permanently posted at the angle on the inner side, and early in the year the defence was further strengthened by posting an additional sentry outside. This fact had an important bearing on the history of the tunnel.

The wall had a postern gate (D) just opposite the orderlies' entrance. This, of course, was always kept locked. It was in any case impossible to get at without either jumping from the end window of the corridor and braving No Man's Land, or cutting the wire near its point of junction with the end of the building by the orderlies' door.

CHAPTER IV

ESCAPES

Such, in brief, were the precautions of the Xth Army Corps for our safe custody: bolted ground floor windows; wire in abundance; an encircling belt of No Man's Land searched to its uttermost inch by strong electric lamps; an absence of any ground that could by a stretch of imagination be termed "dead"; police dogs and night patrols; and withal a very formidable cordon of sentries both within and, subsequently, without the camp. It was not an easy nut to crack by the overland route.

After the original mode of exit—through the Kommandantur in "A" House and out through the main gate—had become known, and therefore obsolete, more direct methods were practised, with, in many cases, great bravery and ingenuity, but in all a regrettable absence of success. Three of these escapades are perhaps deserving of especial mention.

The first[1] of these will always be regarded by those who saw it or knew of it as the bravest and at the same time the coolest exploit of their prison experience. Both the officers who performed it were subsequently killed —in an attempt, it was said, to break away from their

[1] To Lieutenant Fitzgerald of the Australian Flying Corps and his companion—if either of them should read this—my apologies. They were the first men out from Kaserne B at Holzminden, cutting the wire opposite the orderlies' entrance in broad daylight and getting as far as Munster in mid-winter before recapture. But unfortunately I do not know any further details of their escapade.

Scene of the Walter-Medlicott attempt.

A dining-room at Holzminden.

guards after recapture following an escape from Bad
Kolberg. Unfortunately the English version of that
story will never be known, and the sworn evidence of
the sentries—that the British officers, after being delivered over to their escort, and in spite of the most
stringent warnings, broke away and were mortally
wounded in doing so—remains, even if it be true, cold
comfort to their friends. It was the custom that an
attempt to escape, if resulting in capture, involved
automatic transfer to another camp, and of both
Medlicott and Walter, the heroes of this exploit, it
can be safely said that neither of them ever stayed
anywhere in Germany long enough to worry about
making themselves comfortable. Truly a proud record.

On a Sunday afternoon in March the usual sort of
things were happening. There was the usual small knot
of people round the stoves in the Kaserne B cook-house.
There were the usual few taking their afternoon consti-
tutional up and down on the cobbles or round and round
on the cinder. There was the usual bored sentry moving
up and down on his particular beat in No Man's Land
in the stretch between the two Kasernes. Except to
the favoured few in the secret, there was the usual
complete absence of life or interest in the sombre enclosure.

From the shadow of the cook-house two officers,
wearing civilian disguise and carrying bulging rucksacks,
walked steadily over the cobbled track, through the
plain wire fence, across No Man's Land, and up to the
wired railings which formed the northern boundary of
the camp, and which can be seen in the left of the
photograph. Those who were there to see them gave

one gasp of amazement, and then directed an agonized look in the direction of the sentry. He was nearing the lee of Kaserne A, still on the outward portion of his beat, and was not due to turn for another fifteen seconds or so. They pushed their packs through the interstices of the palings on to the road, Walter shinned up the palings, cut the strands of barbed wire, threw back the cutters to accomplices waiting in the enclosure, and dropped into the road. Medlicott followed. Then they assumed their packs and pulled out their civilian hats. As the sentry turned on his beat, two unassuming pedestrians were to be seen walking up the road which ran parallel to the camp towards the railway crossing and the south-east. Fortune so far had favoured this amazing and wonderfully calculated audacity—a scheme worked out literally in terms of seconds. The sentry at the far corner of Kaserne B had also clearly suspected nothing: doubtless his beat had been as carefully observed and timed as that of the other, and the conclusion arrived at that for a given number of seconds the whole length of that particular side of the camp would probably not be under German observation.

Neither would it have been, but for a coincidence against which no calculations or precautions could have been proof. The German cell attendant—a decent little man in his way, but very much *de trop* on such an occasion as this—happened to be looking out of one of the Kaserne B cell windows which gave upon the road, and recognised both Walter and Medlicott, who had only just completed the sentence of confinement incurred for their last escape. He rushed upstairs and gave the alarm. The fugitives, who were by then only a few

yards clear of the camp, realised that something un-
foreseen had marred their plan and that they must run
for it. In broad daylight, and with a hue and cry in
their rear, they stood but the slenderest chance of
making cover in the woods, to reach which they had
first to cross the railway. It being Sunday afternoon,
there was more than the usual traffic on the road and
round the adjoining fields, and—to cut off their one
avenue of escape the more completely—the custodian
of the level crossing had received a prompt warning
from the Kommandantur by telephone as to what he
might expect; and he now stood in the path of the
fugitives with a loaded gun.

So the game was up, and the brave pair were brought
back amidst sympathetic cheers from the windows of
Kaserne B; the cell attendant got three months' leave
on the nail; and Niemeyer, glowing with patriotic
fervour and pride at his still unblemished record, allowed
one of his sentries to shoot without the veriest shadow
of justification at one of the crowded end-corridor
windows of Kaserne B. Fortunately no one was hurt
either by the bullet or the broken glass. But for the
second time in the history of the camp a court of
enquiry sat to examine into a charge of manslaughter
attempted without any provocation. The findings of
this court were ultimately themselves found by the
Germans during a search and promptly confiscated.

Another attempt to escape partook of the serio-comic.
There had been introduced one day into Kaserne B a
length of timber, intended by the authorities to serve
as a framework for messing cupboards in one of the
dining rooms. This timber was, however, promptly

earmarked for a purpose more directly in the interests of the allied cause. A certain beardless professor of astronomy, who had lectured to us the previous Sunday on the wonders of the moon and stars, conceived the idea of projecting himself on this length of timber from one of the corridor windows of the first floor on to the wire of the palisade, and thence to the road beyond. The timber was calculated—and proved—to be just long enough to rest on the wire. His idea was to get himself pushed out on the plank on a sufficiently dark night, and, when the wire was reached, jump for it. Three miles of the Cresta run could not equal this little journey for condensed excitement.

But unfortunately, though it was a dark night and the stage was well set for the adventure, the accomplices pushed too hard, and the extemporised chute—with the professor—went flying into space on the wrong side of the wire, to the intense alarm of the nearest sentry. Next morning the dining room was locked, on the ground that it had been put to improper use. Thereupon several hungry men who wanted to get at their day's food-supply battered in the door with stools. Niemeyer retaliated by locking the whole of the Barrack up within the Kaserne for twenty-four hours. This was a good example of the collective punishments which used so often to be applied in prison camps under the rules of the Hague Convention, embodied, unfortunately, in our own Manual of Military Law. They were futile, served no effective or precautionary end, and succeeded merely in rousing even in the more stolid the most bitter feelings of personal antagonism. It need not be added that such intervals were infinitely more to

Niemeyer's taste than were the humdrum periods of chronic dislike and discontent fostered under his genial charge.

In this particular instance the siege was lifted after twenty-four hours. A draft letter to the *Kriegsministerium*, asking in plain German whether, as the result of one officer attempting to escape, the remaining officers were to be denied access to their food, was presented to the Commandant. Niemeyer saw that he had gone far enough, arranged to parley, and eventually capitulated; an active boycott of the canteen in A Kaserne may also possibly have hastened his resolution.

To the end we never discovered the degree of pecuniary interest which Niemeyer exercised in the profits of the canteen—probably fairly considerable; he at all events never let a chance slip of attesting before all and sundry that he was out of pocket on it.

There was one other very clever attempt made about this time—the only occasion besides the Walter-Medlicott affair on which the wire was successfully cut and negotiated in broad daylight. This again was the result of minute observation and carefully timed and cool action, and the cause of its failure could have been as little foreseen.

The performers in this attempt were Captain Strover (Indian Army), Lieutenant Bousfield (Royal Engineers), and Lieutenant Nichol (R.F.C.). They chose what was perhaps the weakest spot in the cordon of sentries— just behind the parcel room. The back of the parcel room—itself strictly out of bounds except during receiving hours—abutted closely on to the outer wire, which consisted of wire netting at the bottom and barbed strands on top to a height of eight feet. Once through this, and provided you had not been observed, it was only necessary to walk airily through the married quarters, out of an open gate, and into the suburbs of Holzminden town.

The three managed to secrete themselves in the parcel room till about mid-day, when the German personnel betook itself to the most important task of the twenty-four hours. Then, with extreme skill and presence of mind, an aperture in the wire netting was made to admit of the passage of their persons and packs, and was closed behind them in such a way as to leave no trace, except upon minute observation, that the wire had been tampered with at all. The solitary sentry on that particular beat saw nothing, and they walked unchallenged into Holzminden, intending to cross the Weser at the town bridge and make north-west for Holland. But at a street corner they came face to face with one of the tin room attendants of the camp, who knew Strover by sight. He allowed them to pass unchallenged, but a little later obviously thought better of it; and from that moment they were aware that their footsteps were being dogged. They hurried on as fast as was possible, but the game was up. In an incredibly short time, so it seemed, the whole of Holzminden was following them, as the children of Hamelin, further down the Weser, once followed the Pied Piper; and after one half-hearted attempt to disarm suspicion by a mild *was ist los ?* ("what's up ?")— the most appropriate German remark under the circumstances—they chucked their hand in and acknowledged defeat.

It was a striking tribute to the skilful nature of this escape that the hole in the wire was not discovered, in spite of the most elaborate search, till several hours later.

Many other attempts were made, but they were still-born in disaster before the wire was reached: they were made usually at night, and we would be awakened out of our beauty sleep by shouts and tramplings, alarums and excursions, a mild barrage of rifle shots, the flash of a torchlight on to our beds by a harassed Feldwebel conducting an emergency *appel*, and general vituperation after the manner of the best disciplined army in the world.

One bright spirit conceived the idea of parachuting himself on a windy night with an improvised umbrella from the top floor; but either the wind never reached the required velocity, or else his courage—very excusably—ebbed before the sticking point.

Two others tried to be conveyed out of the camp gates in the muck cart which cleared the camp refuse once in every week. The British orderlies on this fatigue were let into the secret, and as soon as the two officers had crept unperceived by the German sentry into the well of the cart, they were engaged to shovel on to and over them the whole of the unsavoury contents of the refuse bin. It was a sporting venture. To sit possibly for hours at the bottom of a heap of decayed food, lees of tea, used tins, and discarded dish-cloths, on the off-chance of being able to get away when the cart was finally unloaded at the town refuse heaps—the ordinary man blenched at the very proposition. Nevertheless it was only bad generalship which prevented them at least from getting clear of the camp. One officer successfully negotiated his part of the programme and was well hidden away in the cart which was clearing the A Kaserne bin. His partner, however, was noticed by the sentry and the alarm was given; with the result that after much prodding and mild comedy each unfortunate was finally unearthed from his malodorous retreat and the pair were marched off to the cells, taking the bathroom en route as a necessary preliminary.

The star of Niemeyer was in the ascendant. Every fruitless attempt increased his arrogance and intensified his bar-tender style of buffoonery. The devil himself when the alarm was on, he could afford to jest and be merry at our expense as soon as the damage had been put right and the tally of his charges agreed once again with the official register.

"Yentlemen," he would say, strutting up to a group of us as we were discussing the Strover episode, "you have taught me a lesson. I shall not forget it. You need not trouble any more. Good morning."

Or some officer of field rank, but just out from five weeks' cells for his last attempt, would be lolling listlessly about, gazing blankly on the horizon and freedom. To him Niemeyer suddenly appearing would proffer unsought advice:

"It is no good, Colonel, you cannot do it: I see to it, you know!"

And pass on, before the other had time to reply.

Or he would stroll up to a knot of officers and discuss bootshops in Bond Street, and express his regret that he should in all probability never visit London again...he had been very fond of London. What a pity

it all was. But then he was only a poor captain and
had to carry out his orders; if only the British would
give their "honour word" not to escape he would order
the wire to be removed immediately.

The best man to deal with him in these moods was
one "Broncho." Broncho, indeed, never failed to tell
the Commandant exactly what he thought of him, and
was a privileged person to that extent.

"It's no good talking like that, Commandant," he
would say. "This camp's a disgrace even to the Xth
Army Corps, and you know it."

And Niemeyer would strut away, hugely pleased.

But these moods were few and far between, and made
him the unreliable blackguard that he was. For weeks
at a time we would be denied the privilege of seeing
his bulky figure in the inevitable blue greatcoat, swaggering along, hands in ·pockets, cigar in mouth, and cap
well on the back of his head; during these periods he
sat tight in the recesses of the Kommandantur and put
out the tentacles of his power through his various
minions. He was reputed to have bouts of drink and
drugging and to hold wild orgies in his comfortable
apartments. Rumour credited him with having been
seen vomiting on to the courtyard from an upper window,
supported on either side by Welman and Ulrich. Certain
it is that his eight o'clock outbursts above related were
confined almost entirely to these periods of segregation
and suggested forcibly the morning after the night
before.

He had, moreover, succeeded in ridding himself of
successive leaders of the opposition. Wyndham, who
as senior officer had fought him tooth and nail, week

in, week out, ever since the Hänisch interview, had been at length transferred to Freiburg, and was recuperating in the milder Baden atmosphere. The breezy Bingham, who succeeded Wyndham in office, fought him at the rate of about three pitched battles a week for a month, and was then transported at two hours' notice to distant Schweidnitz in Silesia. Bingham endeavoured to force the issue on the canteen question, and accused Niemeyer openly of countenancing—if not of fixing—unfairly high prices. The Commandant, almost speechless, challenged him to produce concrete evidence within twenty-four hours, or be court-martialled. Bingham the same day was prepared with chapter and verse, evidence sworn threefold, and damning price lists from other camps. Niemeyer then characteristically refused an interview, and Bingham went the next day. It happened to be one of the days on which B House were locked into their barrack in expiation of some microscopic or imaginary offence; and they gave vent to their feelings by cheering their late senior officer, as he left the camp, loud enough and long enough for the citizens of Holzminden to suspect either that Niemeyer had been assassinated or that we had won the war.

That was the end of Bingham. His successor was of a less militant stamp and things were allowed to drift on in their existing unsatisfactory state. There was one brighter spot. Von Hänisch was induced to make a grudging semi-official recantation about the parole business and we went out for walks again.

CHAPTER V

ACCOMPLICES

BUT to return to our moles and their burrowings.

Attention had, from the start of the tunnelling scheme, been directed to the subterranean parts of Kaserne B. Kaserne A had, for the purposes of a tunnel, been ruled out for various reasons. For one thing, the personnel of the working-party as originally constituted belonged almost exclusively to Kaserne B. For another, Kaserne B was in itself the building more favourably placed geographically for such an attempt. Kaserne A was for half its length Kommandantur ; its "business end" was out of reach for the English.

Accordingly, the basement corridor of Kaserne B was studied in all its aspects. It will be remembered that this floor contained the detention cells and the various cellars, that it was entered at each end of the building through a door at the bottom of a short flight of steps, and that half way down the corridor itself were two doors usually locked. It will be clear, perhaps, that the business end of the building from the escape point of view was bound to be the far end, and that the best base of operations would be somewhere underground in the vicinity of the orderlies' entrance. Owing to the near presence of the detention cells and the consequent risk of meeting the gaoler at awkward moments it would be useless to enter the corridor at the officers' end. It would be necessary to make acquaintance with the underworld by going in the first instance through the orderlies' entrance. Thence some part of the basement floor might be penetrated, either through the door at the bottom of the steps, or by some other means—to be explained shortly. The door I have mentioned was used only by the Germans and was kept locked. It might be possible to tamper with this lock, but it would have to be done from the outside, at the foot of the staircase.

These points have been laboured, but it is highly essential for it to be understood at the start that the only possible entry to the potential base of operations —except by breaking down the barricade or by burrowing at some point through the reinforced concrete of the actual masonry of the building (a process which would greatly imperil discovery)—lay, in the first instance, through the orderlies' entrance.

I have explained that there was a short flight of steps leading down to the basement floor. This was on the right as you passed the threshold of the entrance door. On the left was the first flight of the staircase leading up to the baggage rooms and orderlies' quarters. To the left of the steps down, and completely blocking up the underneath part of the first flight up, was a palisade of stout upright planks, each about six inches across, a further Boche precaution against undue communication with the cellars.

Just as a dummy key to open the basement corridor door had been completed, somebody had a brain-wave which enabled the whole idea of using the cellar passage at all to be dispensed with. It was conjectured (correctly, as it turned out) that behind these planks there must be some sort of square cellar or chamber not actually in use by the Germans. Two sides of it would be bounded directly by the eastern and southern walls of the Kaserne, the western side by the last cellar in the basement corridor (the potato cellar) and the northern side

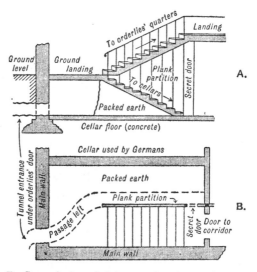

A. Section, B. Ground-plan of staircase, chamber, and tunnel entrance.

by the inside wall of the corridor itself. If this supposition was correct, and if the place could be got at, it would be an ideal spot both as a base of operations for the tunnel and a receptacle for the excavated earth. It was decided therefore, by loosening one or more of the planks and hingeing them so that they could be moved as required in and out of position, to arrange a makeshift but effective trap-door for the daily needs of the working-party.

The ceremony at the laying of the foundation stone —one should say, perhaps, removing the foundation plank—was not largely attended. For one thing, there were at that time only about four people in the know at all ; for another, a German sentry was standing on guard immediately outside the door. Two officers in orderlies' clothes were responsible for the whole operation. They removed *the whole of the partition*, loosened the two necessary planks and replaced it.

The structure of planks fitted very closely against the side and top, except for one place at the top of the plank nearest to the corner post of the partition next to the cellar floor and immediately under the concrete of the staircase, where there was a small aperture looking like a misfit of the boards. Just under this aperture— and on the inside, of course, of the partition—the bolt was fixed. A small hand could just reach the bolt comfortably from the outside and slide it in and out of the corner post. Had the aperture been ever so little smaller, no male hand could have got in at all, and, in the absence of female society, the conspirators would have had either to give up this entrance altogether or increase the size of the aperture, which would have been most dangerous.

By using this door as a means of entrance to and exit from the chamber which, as will be explained later, proved to exist behind the planks, the original party of conspirators succeeded in beginning a tunnel. They dug through the southern foundation wall of the building, turned east at right angles and succeeded by about

Christmas in reaching a point beyond the outer wall[1]. A square chamber was made at the far end of the tunnel, then about 15 yards long, to receive the earth of the roof on the occasion of the escape, and all was ready for a move when Niemeyer suddenly put a sentry *outside* the outer wall, almost on top of the proposed site of exit.

Just at this time the exchange of P.O.W. to Holland began to operate. To some of the original conspirators, disheartened—and no wonder—at the apparent complete frustration of all their plans, the chance of going to Holland seemed too good to be given up for the now very distant hope of escape, and so it came about that the "ownership" of the tunnel changed hands almost completely, only three of the original conspirators remaining in the firm.

As all doors were locked just before dusk, the available time was necessarily limited to daylight, between nine o'clock roll-call in the morning and evening roll-call about an hour before dark. The actual working hours were considerably shorter. In the first place, the coast was never sufficiently clear in the morning for the tunnel to be approached until about 11.30 a.m., and in the second place, a considerable margin had to be allowed, when coming off duty, for any possible delay in getting a clear exit and so running the risk of being discovered absent from *appel*. In addition to this, the time spent in changing clothes had to be taken into account. Consequently the actual working hours were not, as a rule, longer—in winter—than from 12 noon to 4 p.m. This arrangement, however acceptable to a trades union official, was not good for tunnelling. As

[1] Point *Q* in plan on p. 53.

will be understood, the utmost care had to be exercised in approaching the orderlies' entrance in order to gain access to the tunnel, and the ordinary daily programme was carried out on something like the following lines.

We will assume that it is about 11 a.m.

The party of three on duty for the day assemble in a little room on the ground floor and near the officers' entrance. They then take off their uniforms and slip on the black trousers with yellow stripes, the black coats with yellow armlets, and the black caps with yellow bands, which form the distinctive dress of all "other ranks" prisoners-of-war in Germany. Probably greatcoats are put on as well, for it would be highly inconvenient if a German came in just at this moment and wanted to know the why and wherefore of this change of attire. Meanwhile, one or more fellow-conspirators are standing outside the officers' entrance, watching for the "all clear" signal from one of the faithful orderlies standing in their own door-way, who, in their turn, are waiting for some Germans working down in the cellars to clear out for their mid-day meal. Possibly there is a hitch on this particular morning; the stolid German is working later than usual in the cellars at that end of the building. Possibly the German may knock off work before his accustomed time and the signal may be given earlier than usual. But quick or slow, the signal comes in due course—one of the orderlies comes out and scratches his head, the sign that all is clear at his end. The officer on picket duty at the officers' entrance casts one quick look round to see that no Boches are approaching from the direction of the

Kommandantur, and then goes to the room in which the party are waiting and tells them to move. Then he returns to his post to continue his watch until the party are safely on their way and he gets a further signal from the orderlies' doorway that they have actually entered the tunnel.

The three in the little room shed their overcoats, don their orderlies' caps, and sally forth trying to look as much like the British Tommy off duty as is possible under the circumstances. This is the "umpteenth" time for them, and much practising has made them reasonably good actors in the part. Often, however, an additional embarrassment is provided in the shape of a parcel of timber for strutting the roof of the tunnel or a bundle of tin tubes to lengthen the air pipe.

Arrived at the orderlies' door, they enter and stand just inside it, out of sight of the sentry whose position —outside the wire just opposite—gives him a good view of the door as he stands still, facing the camp. But it is unusual for the sentry to stand there long, and as soon as he begins to march away, the orderly who is standing in the doorway with one eye on his every movement gives the word, and the party slips quickly down the steps leading to the cellar, where one of the orderlies slides the plank and lets them in. The aperture is less than a foot wide, but they squeeze in somehow. The door is shut and bolted again in a second, and the orderlies, after making sure that all is ship-shape outside the partition, go off and leave the party to their work, where we shall follow them in a little while.

Such was the game of bluff which took place daily on

that little stretch between the doors of Kaserne B for nine long months. Had any of the party been ever recognised and identified, the game would have been up ; any ground for suspicion on the part of the Germans must have led either to the tunnel being discovered or at least the door being kept so closely under surveillance that another plan of getting underground would have had to be devised. But such a contretemps did not occur until three-quarters of the work had been done, seven and a half months from the beginning of it ! And even then the mischief was not fatal to the success of the scheme.

Luck indeed, but perhaps not quite so much a matter of mere luck as might appear at first sight. In the first place, there was the irrefutable law of mathematical probabilities. There were two platoons of Landstürmers detailed for the guard of the camp, and these relieved each other every 24 hours. Each platoon was divided into three relays of about ten men each, who did two hours on and four hours off. The allocation of "beats" varied for each individual sentry every time he went on duty. It might quite likely be a fortnight before the same man occupied the same station opposite the orderlies' door. Add to this the fact that there were 550 British officers and over 100 orderlies in the camp ; that the personnel of both the *Wachshaft* and the prisoners was continually changing ; and that the thoughts of any sentry at this period were more likely to be occupied with memories of meals in the past, with dreams of meals in the future, with the rottenness of the war in general and of Niemeyer in particular, than with the comings and goings and physiognomies of any British prisoners-of-war ; and the conclusion is arrived at that the risk of detection on this account alone was, when all was said and done, comparatively slight.

Yet risk there undoubtedly was from chance recognition, if not by a sentry, by one of the motley crowd which comprised the German personnel of the camp. We have seen that the attendant at the detention cells could remember faces. His comings and goings to and from the cellar floor were extremely irregular and difficult to anticipate; at any moment he might bob up from the cells and plump face to face into the three going to or returning from their shift. The German interpreters were another difficulty. They might come into the enclosure from the Kommandantur at any time, and not infrequently their business led them into the orderlies' quarters. So might the corporal in charge of the officers' baggage room. If such a thing occurred, and was at all likely to synchronise with the passage from door to door of Kaserne B of three officers dressed for no apparent reason in orderlies' clothes, it was the task of the picket on duty to intercept the intruders, dally with them, pilot them on any pretext into securer waters until time had been given to pass the danger signal either to the changing room or to the orderly waiting innocently at the foot of the orderlies' staircase. Sometimes the "all clear" was delayed for hours on this account and a half-day's shift was lost to the cause.

Those not in the know—the vast majority of the camp—used sometimes to wonder why it was that at certain times of the day there were always one or two members of a particular set loafing aimlessly by the officers' entrance of B Kaserne. Some critical people were even heard to remark that they were wasting their time!

Generally speaking, the immunity from scares was wonderful. Wonderful, too, was the dog-like fidelity of the Germans, officers and men alike, to their sacred dinner-hour. It was indeed only on the most exceptional occasions that a German ever came within the enclosure during this period. It is actually on record that no German officer, except on special occasions such as inspection days, search days, or " strafe " days, *ever* did. Even Niemeyer, most active of belligerents in the early hours, was a party to the universal mid-day torpor. About three in the afternoon he would wake up and sally forth for a little potter round the premises; sometimes he came in at the postern gate by the orderlies' entrance, for which, of course, he had a private key. Therein lay danger always.

The fact is that Niemeyer, although no fool, had left the possibility of a tunnel out of his scheme of defence; or rather he must, after mature consideration, have discarded any such undertaking as physically impossible. He had been round and round the camp, viewed it inside and outside in all its aspects, seen every means of entry to the cellar floor blocked, boarded up, or else permanently watched, and had come to the conclusion that below the surface at any rate he was absolutely secure against attack.

He did not realise, as undoubtedly he should have done—being, as he said, a man of the world and priding himself on his intimate knowledge of the British—that, given time and sufficient freedom from observation, holes could be made without battering rams and tunnels without the proper tools; that he was himself too unpopular with his own people to depend upon clockwork execution of his orders; and that most of his own cowed staff and every German civilian who knew much about Holzminden camp were only too willing—for quite a moderate consideration, in the shape of soap, dripping, or chocolate—to contribute indirectly to doing him a bad turn. And here, before we follow our conspirators behind the planks under the staircase, it will be well to describe these various agents, the bureaux to which they repaired with their information, the caches and repositories for the contraband articles which they brought into the camp, and some of the hundred and one devices wherewith dust was thrown in the eyes of authority.

There was a youthful Prussian known as the Letter Boy, and so called because his principal task was the sorting out and distribution of letters. He had a little broken English and a fair amount of French, and he used either language to lament publicly the fact that his nationality was what it was. This young man also acted as the confidential clerk of Niemeyer and was often used by him instead of the official interpreters to take messages and issue orders to individual officers in the camp. Hating Niemeyer as he did only one degree less than Prussia, and being ready to go to any lengths of treachery —which did not involve detection—in return for favours received, he was, as may be imagined, a useful informant. Every morning he would repair to a room on the attic floor of Kaserne A, which was inhabited by five hardened and inveterate escapers, and which was regarded as the distributing centre of escape materials to the entire camp. Here, over a cup of coffee and some biscuits, he would give the latest news from the Kommandantur, e.g. "there was going to be a search, he had seen the telegram ordering it. A new list for Holland had come in from Hanover. Ulrich had had high words with the Commandant on account of the alleged appropriation by Niemeyer of his (Ulrich's) Christmas wine ration. For the last week a Fortnum & Mason's parcel had found its way every day into Niemeyer's kitchen,"—and so on. And he usually turned out to be right. He was a useful lad ; he was asked every kind of leading question and he asked none back. If he was commissioned to buy anything and it was small enough to go into his pocket, he bought and brought it, regularly and punctually. He must have guessed enough of what was going on to be in a position to wreck the entire scheme if he had wanted to. But he remained to the end punctiliously loyal to his disloyalty, and smiled quite complacently at the fullness of the final success.

Then there was the electric-light boy, a sturdy young Frisian who, for some occult reason, had contrived to confine his active service in the war to six "cushy" months on the South Russian front. Theoretically he was Prussian, Pan-German, and all that was horrible ; actually he was friendly and useful, though not, of course, to be trusted to the same lengths as the Letter Boy. He spoke good German and not the villainous dialect which made direct negotiation so difficult with most of the German-speaking personnel of the camp. He was good for any number of pocket electric torches, and an occasional bottle of *Kriegs Cognac*.

Another "string" was the sanitary man—the only

civilian who was allowed into the camp without a sentry to watch his movements. This gentleman kept a wife and family on the adjoining premises and was always ready, in return for services rendered, to enrich his scanty larder with a store of English tins. He was difficult of access, as his duties did not as a rule take him into the buildings, and he was in a terrible funk of being found out; most of his business was transacted in innocent conversation with the orderlies over the state of the refuse bin, or in consultation over a choked-up drain. Ultimately his larder was found too convincingly full of English tinned foods and he disappeared from our midst; but he had contributed his quota.

There was a girl typist in the Kommandantur whom no one ever saw but who conducted a passionate love intrigue with an Australian Flying Corps officer through the agency of letters attached to a weight and collected by an accomplice sentry. Letters outward from the camp were dropped in this way from the window, picked up by the sentry, and so reached their destination in the Kommandantur. The inward mail used to be thrown up by the sentry and caught at the window. Whenever news of general interest was included in the love passages, an excerpt was made and handed to the senior British officer. As the girl worked in the Commandant's office, there was often valuable material in these missives, and she also acted as a check on the information supplied by the Letter Boy. As to the satisfaction got out of the purely personal side of the affair, opinions might vary. An interchange of photographs was considered too risky, and it is believed that neither party to the adventure ever knew what the other really looked like at close quarters!

The orderly-barber had a similar affair, but was found out and banished to a men's camp, forfeiting thereby a comfortable monthly income from cutting officers' hair, and leaving an awkward gap both in the tonsorial staff, of which he was the only really efficient member, and the orchestra, in which he had for many months been the recognised authority on wind instruments.

An obliging canteen attendant, a patriotic Alsatian amongst the parcel room staff, and half a dozen frankly neutral sentries completed the list of what might be called, from our point of view, the German effectives.

The N.C.O.'s—to do them justice—were beyond suspicion. The majority of them would have been infinitely rather on the Western front than in their present uncongenial position. We never attempted to meddle with them, and indeed there was no need.

The interpreters, although in every way friendly and obliging, were too closely occupied with the multitudinous tasks of their daily routine to invite overtures. There were only three of them in the camp; and what with acting as intermediaries in disputes, visiting the cells, distributing letters, and dancing attendance in and out of season on their German superiors, they were the most hard-worked people in the camp and had hardly a minute to call their own.

Adders was a spotty-faced Dusseldorfian with a perpetual smile and a woman's gait, and was regarded generally with perhaps unmerited distrust.

Grau had been interned early in the war at Ahmednagar in India, and would do anything for anybody who came from India and whom he hoped might be instrumental in restoring him one day to his beloved Nilgiris. "I do not care for Germany," he would say; "I do not care for England. My heart is in India." Poor Grau! I wonder if he ever did get back. A good fellow, not of the stuff to make trouble for the British *raj*.

And Wolff was a little cock-sparrow of a Frankfurter Jew, with an accent acquired on the other side of the Atlantic.

They used to come to the theatrical shows and sit enraptured through the most scurrilous and thinly veiled allusions to Niemeyer and other ornaments of the Xth Army Corps. The fact that they were there solely as censors rather added zest to the humour of it. Sometimes, even, they lost dignity. Wolff in particular was not proof against the attractions of the chemical compound which in those days used to pass for Rhine wine; and after one entertainment at which the bottle passed somewhat freely he became violently intoxicated, and was found next morning asleep in an orchard on the other side of the town, having temporarily thrown off the bonds of barrack discipline and made a regular night of it.

The hardened criminals of Room 83 on the attic floor covered equally satisfactorily the traces of their contraband consignments and the tracks of the consigners. To the outward eye there was not a more innocent-looking room in the whole of the two buildings. But hiding-places lurked everywhere. The floor in this as in nearly every other room was, fortunately, straightforward planking laid without bolts or intersections. Once one plank had been loosened and removed, there was a space about five to six inches deep between the planking and the foundation of the floor wherein to store treasure. When one plank had been removed the remainder could be slid up and down at leisure and the whole of the space filled up, if necessary. This practice was universal, and before the end there was hardly a room without its cache, not one of which, in spite of two or three most conscientious and Berlin-inspired searches, was ever discovered.

In this room also there were sliding panels in the walls, false partitions in the cupboards, false bottoms in the drawers. Almost everything that ought to have been solid was hollow.

Here maps were photographed without cameras and developed without solutions; German uniforms were made for use if a suitable opportunity arose; an air pump was constructed out of bits of wood and the leather of an R.F.C. flying-coat; air pipes were made out of old tins; a device was thought out to fuse the electric wires outside; dummy keys were fashioned. It was the temple of the Goddess of Flight.

Room 24, the little room on the ground floor in B House where the working shifts changed into their orderlies' clothes, was almost as complete a mask. The clothes themselves were kept unlocked at the bottom of several British uniforms in a wooden box. If a search came they would have to take their chance of being found; it was impossible to "cache" them afresh under the boards every time that they were returned from actual use.

In this room it was usual to find four or five seated in conclave, in a space officially allotted to two. "Tim Brean" was the owner of the room and had come to be regarded as the doyen and authority amongst escapers in the camp. Tim had had a curious war. He had carried despatches for a fortnight in August and early September of 1914 and had then been taken prisoner at a cross-roads by an ex-Rhodes Scholar of New College. Since then he had spent his time either preparing to escape or being confined for doing so. He had probably been out of more camps, done more solitary confinement, and had on the whole harder luck, than any other prisoner-of-war in Germany[1]. He spoke correct German with a strong Irish accent. The very perfection and thoroughness of his schemes seemed somehow to have militated against their success. In all his time in Germany he had not been actually at large for more than half an hour. He had always been caught—perfectly disguised and by the purest mischance—at the gate or just outside it. He had gone with the first exchange party for Holland, but at Aachen he had announced his intention of coming back to Germany, and had brought back a full report of the proceedings at Aachen and the lie of the land generally—for the benefit of future parties. It was generally understood that an attempt to escape while on the journey to Holland was permissible when in, or on the German side of Aachen, but not when once the party had left Aachen for the frontier. This was Tim all over. When he was not working for his own hand, he was helping others. He disdained such vulgar expedients as tunnels and was now hard at work on his most elaborate scheme of all. He intended to walk out of the main gate through the Kommandantur in a German private's uniform, accompanied by a young

[1] This seems on retrospect a hard saying. Brean is referred to in Captain J. L. Hardy's book *I Escape* (Bodley Head).

curly-haired and dimpled flying officer disguised as his sweetheart. The plot was by now almost mature, and the curls were already growing in a most beautiful and highly suspicious cluster low on the nape of the young man's neck. His name by the way was Sutcliffe.

Room 24 also harboured such of the official documents of the senior British officer and his adjutant as it was unwise to have lying about in the event of a search. One of these was a most damning, authoritative, and complete narrative of the misdeeds of Niemeyer during the first three months of the camp's existence. It was called the Black Book, and was biding its time to be thrust as red-hot evidence into the hands of some superior inspecting official from the *Kriegsministerium*. Unfortunately that opportunity never arrived, and the book did not attain publicity till it was produced in Copenhagen after the Armistice. It then made interesting reading.

CHAPTER VI

IN THE TUNNEL

WE left the trio next for duty in process of disappearing behind the planks, and about to start on their three-hour shift at the face of the tunnel. Let us keep company with them awhile at their difficult and absorbing task.

Tunnelling had at least one great advantage over other methods of escape, that the interest attaching to the actual preparation was able to over-ride, to some extent, the suspense and anxiety as to ultimate success. There was no opportunity to mope. The immediate business was to defeat not only the Boche but Nature too, with all the odds on the latter's side.

The bolting of the wooden partition behind the last of the trio shuts out the day and adds the proper molish touch to the scene. However, what at first appears pitch dark becomes gradually less so, and presently the party can see enough to change their more or less clean orderlies' clothes for the filthy, sodden, mud-stained rags which they wear for work in the tunnel. There are other minor discomforts besides the darkness and the damp. There is an indescribable musty smell produced by a mélange of damp clay and earth, mice, old clothes, and much-breathed air, a smell which you have to go down into the bowels of the earth to get.

The working clothes are soon on, the clean orderlies'

clothes stowed carefully away, and a move is made to the tunnel mouth.

Look at the plan on p. 73 and glean a rough idea of the shape of the chamber and the siting of the tunnel mouth. The ground area is roughly four yards by five. The height varies, for, on the near (Kommandantur) side, the roof consists of the concrete foundation to the first flight of the orderlies' staircase, while on the far side—that next to the Eastern wall of the building—are the cellar steps. The ground level, which is also the roof level at the southern end, is about five feet above the chamber floor.

Into the available recesses formed by this irregular enclosure all the tunnel earth must be stowed away. The hollow under the cellar steps is already full, and so will be the opposite hollow under the orderlies' staircase before the end is reached, for a 60-yard passage through the earth must be displaced somewhere, and it will be a near thing and will require the most careful and economical storage if the displacements can be kept within the narrow cubic space which is all that can be earmarked for them. A passage from the partition door to the tunnel mouth must be preserved at all costs.

The tunnel mouth has been hacked through the main southern wall of the building just where it joins the cellar floor. It issues about three feet below the ground level—immediately underneath the orderlies' entrance—and then bears sharp left in the direction of the outer wall.

Now the outer wall is but ten yards away at this point, and had the original scheme of the tunnel gone as it had been planned, all would have been over long before this particular May day, and the conspirators would have made their bid for freedom. There was nothing very Herculean involved in getting the tunnel to the other side of the wall and popping up on a dark night, with the friendly wall acting as a screen from the view of the nearest sentry.

But unfortunately, as has been explained, Niemeyer had taken precautionary measures just before the party were ready to move, and had put a sentry at the outside corner of the building, effectually covering the spot. Unless this sentry was removed it would be necessary, in order to have a reasonable prospect of success, to continue the tunnel until a point was reached where it would be possible to emerge under cover.

These bald words cannot attempt to convey the bitter disappointment caused by Niemeyer's manœuvre or the seriousness of the altered prospect.

But the Tunnellers of Holzminden set their teeth and prepared themselves, if necessary, to go on digging for a year rather than run the risk that any of the party should be spotted by a sentry as he emerged. It was known how many a previous tunnel scheme had been shattered miserably on this rock, simply through lack of the necessary patience to go on with the job. At Schwarmstedt, not so many months before, this had happened. The tunnel came out quite close to the wire. One officer got out and got away, but in so doing was observed by a sentry. His successor had no sooner put his head above ground than he was shot dead in the most cold-blooded and treacherous manner—legitimately murdered, if one may venture on the paradox.

There was a road immediately beyond the outside

wall, and the ground beyond the road was planted with low-growing crops and vegetables over a belt of about 40 yards in breadth. The whole of this belt was searched by the glare from the strong electric lamps at the corner of the wall. Day and night there was now a sentry outside the wall. If Niemeyer had posted machine guns at intervals of 50 yards round the camp, he could hardly have felt more immune from attack, more absolutely secure from any attempt to spring him by the tunnel method.

It was early days—in April—to offer any decided opinion as to what the vegetables were likely to be. If they turned out to be crops which were not high enough to offer adequate cover to the escapers, there would be no choice—as the sketch will show—but to tunnel grimly on till the ryefield was reached, several yards further away. But the rye would be cut in early August at latest, and meanwhile the tunnel had advanced barely ten yards beyond the outside wall, and at best a two-foot progress crowned during this period the effort of each laborious day. This meant about 40 yards still to tunnel and three months to go in a losing race, probably, unless progress could be accelerated; and this, as the work took the party further and further from their base, was hardly to be expected.

So it is with the depressed feeling of having to work against time as well as nature that our friends assemble behind the partition on this particular morning. They are standing, or rather stooping, at the entrance, and the first thing to do is to light up. Fortunately someone has remembered to bring the matches to-day, so Number 1 lights a couple of precious candles (we were

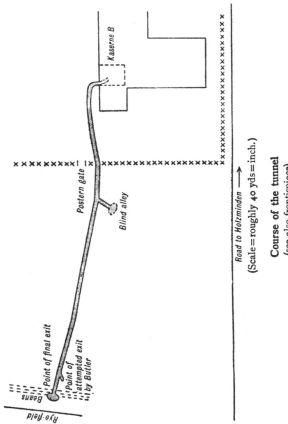

Course of the tunnel
(see also frontispiece).

dependent entirely on England for these commodities) and crawls in. He sticks one candle in the pump chamber, which is just round the first corner and about six feet from the entrance, and proceeds on his way with the other. His progress is necessarily slow, very slow, as the tunnel is so small that he is compelled to *wriggle* along on his elbows and toes. There is no help for this. The hole must be as small as possible, because of the extreme economy to be exercised in the disposition of the displaced earth.

Number 2 enters the pump chamber and starts working the pump. This instrument consists of a home-made vertical bellows, manufactured from wood and from the leather of a flying coat, and is operated by Number 2 with his left hand as he sits facing it and looking along the tunnel towards the face. The pump is screwed to wooden uprights which are securely embedded top and bottom in the clay soil, and the air is forced into a pipe composed of tin tubes made out of biscuit boxes. Little did the glorious company of biscuit makers suspect that in sending us our means of sustenance they were also contributing to an important escape. This pipe is sunk in the floor of the tunnel and is kept always close to the face by the addition of more and yet more tubes.

Number 3, whose duty it will be to pack the earth when it is hauled out, stays outside the tunnel mouth and sees that the rope attached to the basin is running clear, and then hands the basin to Number 2, who puts it in front of him ready to be pulled to the face by Number 1 with that half of the rope which extends from the pump chamber to the face. We shall see what the basin was for if we accompany Number 1 on his journey to the tunnel face.

For the first few yards he goes down a slight slope, then again for a few yards up an incline to the place where it was originally intended to make the exit—just beyond the boundary wall. Here he can hear the thud-thud of the sentry's footsteps above his head. Then he goes down again pretty steeply for three or four yards and flattens out, the tunnel swinging slightly, first to the right and then to the left. All this time he has been going through fairly soft stuff—a sort of sandy yellow clay, which has been easy enough to dig—but now he comes to the stony part. Working in this stretch has been terribly difficult. A dense, seemingly interminable stratum of large stones has been encountered. The stones are smooth and flat, tightly pressed together in a horizontal position and cemented with the stickiest of clay. Number 1's progress becomes positively painful: he barks his shoulders on the stones which project from the walls, his toes and elbows suffer from the stones beneath him, occasionally he bumps his head on the uneven roof, and all the time he must keep the candle alight, and swear only in an undertone. Soon he begins to ascend again—steeply this time—and comes to the face, but not before he has had yet one more unpleasant experience. Out of the gloom in front of him appears suddenly a pair of wicked little eyes, horribly bright and menacing. He clenches his teeth and digs his chin into the soil beneath him. The large rat, whose solitude he has disturbed, crawls over him and leaves him sweating with fright and almost faint with the eerie sensation of it

But the tunnel must go on, so Number 1 sticks the candle on some convenient stone at his side, takes the cold chisel and gets to work. In five minutes or less he has loosened a bathful of stones and he drops the chisel, takes hold of his end of the rope and hauls. The difficulties of hauling on a rope while lying in a tube about eighteen inches in diameter lined with knobbly stones can be imagined but cannot be adequately described. Soon he hears the rattling of the basin on the stones behind him, and it arrives at his feet. Next comes the contortionist's trick of getting it past his body in the confined space, then the filling, and finally the almost superhuman juggling feat of getting the full basin back past his body again. A couple of jerks at the rope leading to the pump chamber, and he feels it tauten. The basin begins to move away, and Number 1 turns on to his side again and gets to work, taking care that he has the *end* of the rope attached to some part of his person but that the rest of it is free.

If he is a fairly quick worker, he will have another load of stones ready by the time the basin has been pulled back and emptied. He will then haul it up again and repeat the whole exhausting process. No wonder that the tunnel party did not as a band shine as games enthusiasts amongst their fellow-prisoners. They had their bellyful of exercise down below.

Sometimes the monotony of the proceedings is varied by a torrent of subdued cursing from the pump chamber, while the full basin is on its way back. To the experienced this only signifies that the rope has broken, as it frequently does on account of the damp and the incessant friction against the sides, roof, and floor of the tunnel.

A breakage entails a journey on the part of Number 2 to effect repairs while Number 3 pumps.

The working time is divided into three equal parts, and at the end of the first part Number 3, who is time-keeper as well as packer, informs Number 2. A low hail informs Number 1 that his digging is over for the day, and he retraces his steps—or more accurately wriggles back feet foremost, for there is no room to turn round. He then becomes Number 3, Number 2 becomes Number 1 and goes to the face, whilst Number 3 becomes Number 2 and pumps.

So the work goes on till 3.45 p.m. Then it ceases; all three come out of the tunnel and change back into their orderlies' clothes to await the signal to come out. At the orderlies' entrance to the building stand two of the orderlies waiting for a favourable opportunity to let them out, and, just as during the morning manœuvre, there are two or three officers loafing about for no apparent reason at the other end of the building. On some days there are no Boche about at this time and immediate exit is possible, but to-day they happen to be carrying potatoes down to the adjoining cellar, and pass to and fro close to the hiding-place, quite plainly visible through the cracks in the boards. They could not see anything, naturally, even if they thought of looking, as they are in the light and the chamber is practically in the dark.

At last they go. "Come out now," sings out one of the orderlies, looking skywards and as if singing a snatch of a music-hall song from sheer light-heartedness. The trio unbolt the plank door and, slipping quickly to the top of the steps, stand just inside the orderlies' door, precisely as they had stood in the morning with the day's work in front of them; and an orderly waiting for a moment at the bottom of the steps fastens the secret door. The orderly standing at the entrance looks down the enclosure to make sure that no Germans are about, and then says "Right." Off they go again. If the sun is shining, the light is very dazzling after the darkness.

At the last moment, perhaps, and when home is so nearly reached, a German Feldwebel appears from nowhere in particular and heads for the same door. Out from the cookhouse, which stands just opposite the officers' door, walks one of the aimless, lounging, loafing officers above mentioned, and delays the Feldwebel with some question, no matter how trivial. So home is safely made again, and the party become officers once more and put off their orderlies' clothes. Then follows *appel*, and the joy of a good wash in hot water and something to eat.

The hours have not been long, but the foul atmosphere has caused considerable fatigue, perhaps a bad headache. And in case anyone should still think, after reading this, that the work was light, he should be invited to wriggle 50 yards on elbows and toes *in the open*, and if he is unduly sceptical, in public. He will lose dignity, but he will gain an appreciation of the difficulties of the performance in a very confined space.

· · · · · · ·

There are a few other points in regard to the construction of the tunnel which may not be without interest.

When and where necessary, the roof was revetted. The revetting was done with bed boards. The foundations of all beds in the camp were boards placed cross-wise across an iron frame and supporting a mattress made of paper, straw and shavings, and uneven as the Somme battlefield. Many of these boards had been commandeered as firewood during the early stages of the camp, when there had been, as related, a regrettable hitch in the arrangements for our warming. Many more now found their way underground by driblets into the orderlies' quarters and thence into the recess behind the planks, or were carried direct by the working-party. People clamoured querulously for the missing boards which they had saved from the burning, and of which they had now been robbed. No one except the very few in the secret and an orderly or so had the ghost of a notion what had really happened to them. The Boche when appealed to of course shrugged their shoulders and quoted the equivalent German proverb about eating your cake. What would you? Very nearly all is fair in escapes.

The only tools used in the digging of the tunnel were a trowel or "mumptee" (an instrument with a spike at one end and an excavating blade at the other) and the cold chisel. The chisel was useful for levering apart the smooth heavy stones which presented so much difficulty. It seems probable that these stones had once formed the bed of some river and had been worn smooth and packed by the action of the water. Attempts were made to dodge this difficult stratum of stones which retarded progress so seriously, but in the absence of proper instruments it was impossible to gauge the level with any degree of accuracy. A descent of four feet bringing no better results, it was decided to come back to the previous level of about eight or nine feet below the surface.

The chamber was just—and only just—sufficient for the earth. When the last sackful[1] had been piled the chamber was practically full of earth from floor to ceiling and in every crevice.

Orientation was not an easy matter. It was necessary of course only to bear in a general easterly direction as straight as possible. There were rough compasses galore in the camp, but it was very difficult to dig the tunnel straight and the compasses were too small to check errors accurately.

Towards the end the tunnel had become too twisted and hilly to permit any longer of the rope and basin method being used, and it was necessary to fill sacks and drag them back from the face. This method was even more wearisome and exasperating than the other. To wriggle back by oneself was bad enough: to wriggle back, and every yard or so pull a heavy sack after one, was infinitely more so. Nevertheless, all this practice had its advantages: it braced the muscles of the working-party for the great night when each one of them would have to worm his way through the tunnel, pushing a loaded pack in front of him.

[1] See the photograph opposite. The sacks were mostly mattresses stolen from beds and quite unaccounted for also !

At the tunnel mouth.

CHAPTER VII

REPRISALS

THE days wore on, lengthening to the advantage of the cause and permitting of longer shifts. The working-party added to its numbers, allotting a few more privileged places without difficulty; for by now the thing was beginning to be known and discreetly talked about, and founders' shares were at a premium. A few who might have been able to obtain them, but whose turn had come for exchange, were unable to resist the temptation and departed for Holland. The working-party and some others, on being asked their intentions, politely intimated that they preferred to remain in Germany. Had Niemeyer only taken more intelligent stock of the particular quarter from which so many unexpected refusals emanated, it is possible that he might have drawn valuable conclusions.

But Niemeyer, astute German though he was, disregarded these and other even more valuable hints which were to be offered him before the scheme was ripe for launching, and which could have told him easily enough in which quarter the wind blew. As an instance of one, there arose in early June a sudden and curious demand on the part of certain individuals for transfer from A to B Kaserne. Three officers, comfortably situated in a small room in the former house (the same room, by the way, as that in which the Letter Boy used to spend so much of his time), overlooking the picturesque suburbs of Holzminden, and blessed with apparently every comfort that a prisoner-of-war could require, asked unashamedly if they might become one of a motley, closely packed crew in one of the big rooms on the ground floor of B Kaserne. Many of the reasons given for the desire to change were ingenious, but if submitted to anybody with a less cast-iron mould of thought than the German camp officers it is unlikely that they would have convinced. However, change they were allowed to, and change they did; and the working-party of twelve were now all lodged in B Kaserne.

This was a very necessary move for the following reason: when—if ever—the tunnel was used in earnest, it would be used after dark and lock-up. Consequently those who intended to use it would have all to be in B Kaserne at the time. For any less important occasion it might have been feasible for the A house members of the scheme to arrange to change places for the night with accomplices in B house, the A house officers answering to the B house officers' names and *vice versâ*. This used to be done sometimes for occasions such as a birthday party or a theatrical show, when the presence of some member of the other house was essential to the success of the evening's programme. But more often than not it was spotted, and either condoned or reported according to the nature and temper of the Feldwebel taking the *appel*. On a large scale and for an event of the nature of the tunnel, for the success of which complete absence of any suspicion on the part of the Germans was an absolute *sine qua non*, such a risk was not possible, and, indeed, could not be allowed.

It was intended that, whatever happened, and whatever
the hardship that might occur in individual cases, the
night of the escape should not find a single officer in B
Kaserne who was not domiciled there with the permission of the Germans. This intention was happily carried
into effect.

Meanwhile, the owners of the founders' shares, knowing, as they did, pretty well the conditions under which
the scheme was to be submitted to the public, took
time by the forelock and changed houses before the
rush.

It was indeed an undertaking in which the home
policy was fraught with almost as many dangers as the
foreign, and required the most patient and tactful
handling. Fortunately there was only one of the allied
nations in the camp, and this fact of itself quartered the
risk. Inter-allied jealousy, or merely Latin or Slavonic
exuberance, had many a time ere this during the war
wrecked a promising and well-laid plan. But even in a
camp where all were English and the loyalty to the
cause of the whole community never for an instant came
in question, there were yet grave risks of discovery
through some intemperate speech or action of the newly
captured or the not overwise.

It was just after the arrival of one hundred newly
captured officers from the big March offensive of 1918
that the cat was most nearly let out of the bag. A
"show" was on, and the audience were sitting in packed
rows and eager expectancy in front of the curtain,
waiting for the intellectual fare of the evening to be set
forth on the dining room tables. A canteen "boycott"
was in full force at the time, and the company, in the

absence of the bottle that cheers, was comparatively quiet. The Germans used to make so much money out of the English over the wine—and wretched wine at that—that the senior British officer had every now and again to clap on a drastic boycott on the canteen and forbid officers to buy anything there at all. Sometimes this policy was two-edged and as much in the interests of peace and quiet in the camp as to the detriment of German profiteers. At all events you could always tell whether a boycott was on or not by the amount of noise which attended the fortnightly shows, and it so happened that on the particular occasion with which we are concerned you *could* hear your next-door neighbour speak.

Suddenly a padre—one of the new arrivals—leant over to make a remark to an officer sitting near him, and in bell-like tone uttered the dreadful question:

"*Are you in the tunnel?*"

A shiver ran through the whole of the adjoining rows. Two of the German interpreters were seated within two yards.

On another occasion an ingenuous youth was found leaning out of one of the first floor corridor windows and carrying on an animated conversation about escapes, past and future, with one of the occupants of the cells. They were apparently analysing the causes of failure of a recent attempt and discussing the prospects of success of another imminent one. Any English-speaking German who happened to be in the building at the time—it was midsummer, and all the windows were open—could not fail to have been suitably impressed with this dialogue.

A newly captured officer with a bump of observation
startled those near him one day by singing out to a
friend to know whether he too had recognised "these
officers walking about in orderlies' clothes."

The senior British officer did, of course, from time to
time issue stringent orders about the paramount importance of secrecy, and sometimes personally harangued
the occupants of each building. But the difficulty was
to cater for the odd handful—what we used to call "the
elusive half per cent"—who either succeeded in absent-
ing themselves from such harangues or, if present, failed
to understand their purport, and of whom it might fairly
be said that they were so stupid and perverse as to be
a real danger to their own side, on whichever side of
the line. A bump of carelessness, a bump of cussed-
ness, a faulty sense of discipline, and a penchant towards
selfish individualism—when two or three endowed with
these qualities were gathered together, the lot of those
responsible for their actions was not a pleasant one.
The senior officer was powerless, if any chose disloyally
or unintentionally not to support him; he exercised the
authority vested in his person by virtue of King's Regulations, and there it ended. A court of enquiry and a
threat of post-bellum action against the offender was
the limit of his power. Nor was it easy to enjoin general
secrecy on a subject which was never put publicly into
words. Hole, not tunnel, was the word used, if a word
had to be used—and then only in an undertone, or
behind closed doors.

But in spite of these potential sources of leakage,
nothing occurred to mar the progress of the tunnel
until the middle of May, when it had been in full

swing for five and a half months and reached to somewhere about the middle of the vegetables. Then a
bomb-shell fell. It was announced one day on *appel*
that in consequence of measures of reprisals which had
been taken against German officers in a certain camp in
England, counter-reprisals would be put into force in
the Xth Army Corps until further notice. There would
be no less than four *appels* a day, at 9 a.m., 11.30 a.m.,
3.30 p.m. and 6 p.m.; music, theatricals, games, and
walks were to be stopped; and no newspapers were to be
permitted into the camp. The Commandant regretted,
but orders were orders, and so on in the usual vein.

It struck us as deliciously ironical that counter-reprisals on ourselves should be the first outward and
visible sign that anything had come of the agitation
which had, we knew, been raised on our behalf by
influential officers amongst the earlier Holland parties.
It ultimately transpired that strong representations had
been made to the German War Office as to the maladministration in the Xth Army Corps and particularly
in the camps governed by the Twin Brethren, Heinrich
and Karl Niemeyer; when it became clear that no
attention was being paid to these representations, steps
were taken to collect in one camp in England all the
German officers who belonged to Hanoverian regiments
and to deal with them as a measure of reprisals on
appropriate lines. The measure signally failed, after
the manner of reprisals. In the first place, it was impossible to find any Englishman at all like the Niemeyers, and therefore the conditions ruling with us
could not be even approximately reproduced at home;
in the second place, a German government that was as

yet impenitent and still sanguine of ultimate success
decided that their best course lay in prompt counter-
reprisals. One of the features of this "strafe" was that
we were invited to send full accounts of it home in our
letters, provided only that we also mentioned the alleged
reason. An extra letter was offered us in which to do
so[1]. This was a clumsy and typical German device to
endeavour to alienate popular feeling at home. Needless to say, it was seen through, and not a single letter
mentioned the subject at all.

Any alternative to reprisals as a means for one belli-
gerent power to stop the malpractices of another was
not, so far as I am aware, discovered during the war.
But it was a poor arrangement at the best.

The added *appels* had a serious effect upon the out-
put of excavated earth, for the working hours were now
considerably reduced, and there were long faces amongst
the initiate. Those in authority began to have serious
qualms as to whether—even if all went well from now
on—the tunnel would have advanced near enough to
the rye crop before it was ripe for the sickle. Such
local papers as we were now compelled to smuggle into
the camp spoke of an early harvest. Added to this, the
entire camp, having now no games to play and nothing
particular to occupy itself with, began to take notice of
things to which they had been blind hitherto; and an
embarrassing number of enquiries—most secretly and
impressively conducted, but embarrassing withal—
began to be made as to the progress of the unmention-
able thing. Certain people all at once discovered that

[1] Normally we were allowed to write two letters in each month (six sides
to a letter) and four post-cards.

they could in future only support existence if buoyed up by the hope of escape, and began to ingratiate themselves accordingly in the proper quarter. There arose a strong and inconvenient demand for places in what came to be known as the "waiting list," which did not in the least help the progress of what they were waiting for.

During these days of counter-reprisal, which lasted about a month, the event occurred which might so easily have put the lid on the whole scheme, but which did, in fact, probably prove to be its salvation. An officer returning from his shift to the officers' entrance was recognised by a sentry. The sentry reported the episode but could not give the officer's name. Niemeyer quickly appeared on the scene, attended by the camp officers, and conducted a cross-examination and thorough investigation on the spot; and the British were kept standing on *appel*—those of them concerned in an agony of apprehension—until the conclusion of the enquiry.

So well, however, was the entrance to the tunnel concealed, and so inconclusive was the evidence supplied by the sentry, that Niemeyer failed badly to take advantage of the one real clue ever presented to him in the history of the tunnel. He knew the English too well to think for a moment of parading the whole camp before the miserable sentry on the chance of an identification; such an attempt would have meant a crowded hour or so of sheer delight for the British and of baffled exasperation for himself. He ultimately came to the conclusion that if there was anything in the sentry's statement there was probably some embryo stunt afoot (in this he was not far wrong); and contented himself with the precaution of placing an additional sentry at the orderlies' door. The conspirators breathed again. All was not yet lost.

When nothing further at all suspicious was reported, the mood of the versatile Niemeyer again reacted, and the informing sentry was given eight days in cells for making a false report. This act, besides being typically unjust, was also one of questionable policy, since it naturally tended to make other sentries uncommunicative of anything suspicious that they might see or hear. Punishment in cells with them was an infinitely more serious affair than it was with us. They had only their own miserable ration and were cut off even from the slender assistance of the home parcels on which most, if not all of them, relied to keep their bodies and souls together.

The immediate upshot, so far as the tunnel and the additional sentry were concerned, was that so long as the sentry remained posted over the orderlies' entrance the tunnel could not possibly be got at by the previous method. A new entrance to the chamber had to be made, and this was set about at once. A hole was begun through the wall of the last of the big living rooms on the ground floor which adjoined directly on to the chamber. This hole would give entry to the chamber somewhere underneath the staircase flight. It should be explained here that the only reason which had prevented this hole being attempted at a much earlier stage in the proceedings was the obvious and almost certain risk of any such hole being discovered in a search and thereby ruining the whole scheme. Only the present desperate state of affairs justified the risk being taken at all.

The inhabitants of Room 34 (the big room in question) had, of course, to be let into the secret, if secret it could any longer be called. One member of the patrol now sat in a deck-chair at the end of the corridor just opposite the door of the room, whence he could command the whole length of the passage and dart in at once to warn the workers inside if any German hove in sight. A different officer every hour sitting at this particular spot in the corridor, reading a book and apparently perfectly resigned to the discomfort of the site and the disturbance to his reading caused by the perpetual traffic—if the Germans who did occasionally come along had stopped for a moment to think....

But the fact is that the reprisals were militating for us as well as against us. The German personnel were not enjoying the counter-reprisals any more than we were; counting 250 officers five times a day, even in the most superficial manner, was a task that was obviously trying the patience of both the Feldwebels and the Lager officers very severely, and it is not surprising that during this period they left us well alone when they were given the opportunity. On the argument that both sides had a grievance, personal relations between the British and Germans (with the exception, of course, of Niemeyer) improved by leaps and bounds; and the supervision was more cursory and the letter of the law more loosely interpreted than at any previous time in the camp's history.

The then senior British officer, Colonel Rathborne, D.S.O., was himself deeply interested in the success of the scheme, and had, in fact, been offered a place immediately after the original working-party. It was his

obvious policy to foster as much as possible the existing
state of good relationship and to avoid serious collision
with the authorities. Consequently the reprisals were
left to work out their own sweet course; Niemeyer was
ignored; when a hammer disappeared from the tool-
bag of a civilian carpenter working in the camp and the
Feldwebel-Lieutenant Welman demanded its instant
restoration on pain of a general search, the hammer was
immediately produced. A German tin room attendant
had his cap whisked off his head by some adventurous
and unidentified spirit. The threats of a general search
were repeated, and the cap as promptly restored. The
Jewboy and the Germans generally were welcome to
draw any conclusions they wished as to our impaired
morale. Their conclusions were of secondary importance.
But a general search at such a time would have been a
disaster of the first magnitude, and Room 34 could
hardly have got through with its secret unnoticed.

However, the attempt to make an entry into the
chamber from Room 34 proved abortive, owing to the
difficulty of digging through the solid concrete of the
wall with the available tools. So after desperate efforts
for about a week the deck-chair habit ceased as suddenly
as it had begun, and the working-party turned their
attention to the attic, which was now the one remaining
available avenue of approach.

Leading to the attic floor from the officers' staircase
were two swing doors. As the attic floor had now been
placed altogether out of bounds for officers, these doors
were padlocked and secured by a chain which passed
through the two large loop-handles of the doors. The
doors were forced by unscrewing one of these handles,

which were fastened by six screws through their bed-plates. The screws had to be replaced every time the conspirators went in or out. Entry was then possible into one of the now disused officers' small rooms. A hole was knocked through the wall of this room into a space between the wall of the attic, the roof, and the eaves, thus:

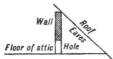

This space communicated with the orderlies' quarters by means of a small door which had been built into the house to permit of access to the eaves. The hole in the vacant room was camouflaged with a bit of board, cut to size and covered with glue on which was sprinkled mortar and distemper to tone with the wall of the room.

The use of this room as the means of access to the orderlies' quarters, and so *viâ* the staircase and the same old secret door to the tunnel, made up in full for the previous week's delay and immensely accelerated the rate of progress. It was no longer necessary to work by means of carefully timed and well-reconnoitred reliefs; the work could now go on all day and all night, with interruptions only to admit of attendance on *appels*. When the reprisal restrictions were removed, things would go on even more swimmingly; as it was—and in spite of continued trouble with the stones—the tunnel was already estimated to be nosing its way to within measurable distance of the coveted rye.

When the Commandant's suspicion at length subsided and the extra sentry was removed from the orderlies'

entrance, the decision had to be made whether to revert
to the old method of getting to the tunnel or to stay
with the quicker method and risk a search. It goes
almost without saying that the latter counsel prevailed.
It was now mid-June, and with any luck it was hoped
that the tunnel would have been taken far enough by
the first week in July. If they went back to the old
method, it might not be ready before August. At the
worst the Letter Boy, or some other agent, might be
safely relied upon to give 24 hours' notice of a search,
during which time much might be done still further to
conceal the traces of the attempted hole in Room 34—
though this had already been fairly effectually done—
and the actual hole in the attic. But it was unlikely,
since these attic rooms were now out of bounds and the
swing doors apparently securely padlocked, that a search
would extend so far.

It might be asked why had not this decision been taken
before, and why in the early stages the cumbrous method
of approaching the tunnel in orderlies' clothes under the
very nose of a sentry had been preferred. The answer
to this very reasonable question is that three weeks is
not eight months. At this juncture it was reasonable
odds against a search being held before the tunnel was
completed. In November it was all the odds on.
Actually, since operations had been begun, there had
been two searches, both of them—as regards the ground
floor at any rate—extremely thorough. No hole in a
wall could have hoped to escape the sleuth hounds
specially sent down from Berlin for these occasions.
They may have got the worst of it in some of the personal encounters—indeed, they very rarely did discover

any *articles* of a contraband nature; the British officers who owned any as a rule took care not to be collared in possession, and very often the war was carried into the enemies' country and the civilian detectives found, on leaving a room, that they had somehow managed to mislay an umbrella, or a hat, or some other object of civilian attire useful for escapes—all of which, it need hardly be said, provided scope for a most exhilarating exchange of amenities, and sometimes for grave allegations against the moral proclivities of the British prisoners. But with bricks and mortar our black-coated friends were on surer ground, and they would not have needed very high qualifications to have spotted a gaping hole in a wall camouflaged behind a bed. So our Tunnellers had had to go outside to get to their work, and the plank door had been decided upon.

Searches, though they meant confinement to the buildings for the best part of the day and made cooking a decent meal at the stoves impossible, were nevertheless welcomed by all except those who had much to lose and no time to hide it in as a pleasant variation to the monotonous round. For one thing, they introduced for a brief space a foreign element into the camp. Quaint little spectacled civilians from Berlin, full of zeal for their duties for an hour or so, but tiring rapidly as the same ritual was gone through in room after room of polite but mildly amused prisoners, could be induced, with a little persuasion, to talk of food conditions in the capital, their opinion on the war, and other interesting subjects. The full dress uniform of a police officer provided a pleasing variation to the eternal field grey; or some Captain from Hanover, in charge of the company specially detailed for the search, interested simply because his face was new to us.

For any material result, both the searches held at Holzminden were an absolute farce. Of one of them we had full warning. An enormous quantity of books were temporarily confiscated for examination and removed to the parcel room. One or two maps which had been carelessly left uncovered were duly netted; but anything of real importance, such as civilian hats, clothes, compasses, and the overwhelming majority of the maps, were securely hidden before the search ever began, and all that happened was that every officer in the camp was invited to undress and then to dress again. These ordeals were great fun. When it got to the final stages and the victim was in his undergarments, he was invited to give his parole that he had nothing actually concealed about his person. With some of us delicacy conquered. Others were less fastidious and requested the German to continue his ungrateful task to the bitter end. Long before the attic floor—in both houses the richest in contraband stores—was reached, the searching-parties had tired of the beauty of the human form and proceedings had become entirely formal.

One officer prominent in this story was taken by surprise at one of these searches with a whole escape kit under his bed. But he had also at the foot of his bed a large black wooden box which had a double bottom. Luckily, when the sleuths entered his room, the first thing that caught their eye was the big black box. They turned everything out of it and tapped the bottom. After a frenzied argument, lasting quite half an hour, between a detective from Berlin who said there was a double bottom, and the double bottom expert, who, being called over to examine it, said there was not, the former triumphantly put his foot through the false bottom. It hid one or two books (prayer books, etc.) and some private papers of no particular interest. These articles were carried off in triumph, and every Hun present shook the detective's hand as if he had scored a goal for Blackburn Rovers. They were so pleased that they *forgot to look under the bed.*

It should be added that on these occasions the camp personnel could be relied upon to do their utmost in helping to baffle the search. Thus, for instance, a sentry could—for a cake of soap, or a stick of chocolate—be easily induced to act as temporary banker for a large number of German notes of the realm. Feldwebels could be persuaded to give permission for an officer to visit the latrine under guard, well knowing that he had only gone to put something out on short deposit in a reliable quarter. In some cases the Feldwebel was even known to take the risk of the market himself. It was a curious phenomenon, in fact, that on such gala days the camp personnel became infinitely more indulgent than on ordinary working days. It was as if they were disposed to make common cause with us against Niemeyer and his imported mercenaries. In doing so the camp sentries did not forget to help themselves unasked whenever they had an opportunity. Whilst we were shut up in our rooms, they had ample access to the dining rooms; and it was an amusing climax to the day's sport to see the whole of the guard marched off to the parcel room after the search to be themselves searched in their turn, their pockets simply bulging with stolen tins or eatables, and in many cases the delinquents making frantic efforts to eat a two days' supply in two minutes and incur the penalty of indigestion rather than that of nine days' cells for being found in possession of stolen goods. The whole business was rather Gilbertian. I do not think it could have happened in England, even if there had been a famine there.

Niemeyer must have realised the futility of these field-days, for there were no searches held between a date in March and the time of the tunnel escape. On one occasion all the preparations for one had been made, and the information duly passed on through the usual channels to us. But Niemeyer, in his turn, came to know that we knew, and not only cancelled the operations but told us frankly that he had done so. We had sometimes to give the devil his due for a sense of humour.

CHAPTER VIII

THE LAST LAP

AFTER a brief spell of smoother working, both above and below the surface, things began to go wrong again.

In the first place, the exasperating stratum of stones recurred and persisted. The tunnel was now being inclined upwards. From rough measurements it had been estimated that the face must now be approaching the desired spot and be nearly abreast with the edge of the rye-field. But the obstinate stratum added to the difficulty of working uphill, and reduced the rate of progress almost to the lowest on record ; and, work as they might, it was the last week in June before those directing decided that the distance had been accomplished and the tunnel might be inclined to the surface.

On the last day in June Lieutenant Butler, one of the leading spirits in the concern, went up to the face on the important duty of breaking the surface and pinpointing the position. The tunnel had at length been pushed through the clogging stratum, a total ascent of nine feet had been made from the lowest point, and it was judged that the end of it must now be very near the surface. To confirm this, a narrow hole was bored straight upwards from the face. It was found that there were still six feet of clay and soil to be negotiated. This was disappointing, but it was not so disappointing as was the result of verifying the actual position. Butler very gingerly pushed a stick with a piece of white paper attached to it up through the hole. The watchers from one of the upper end-corridor windows groaned as they discerned the damning piece of paper moving slowly to and fro, *still eight or nine yards short of the rye.*

The interest and general tension had now become so great that, although nothing was said, half the camp knew the same evening that something was wrong and guessed fairly shrewdly what the something was. To carry on into the rye would take at least three weeks' hard work, by which time the rye would probably have been cut and the only cover afforded would be the darkness of the night. But about three or four yards nearer than the rye was a row of beans, and it was decided to make a last effort to reach these and to trust to luck and the darkness to carry the party across the bare space between the beans and rye. The beans in themselves would afford no mean screen.

Meanwhile, "Munshi" Gray, another of the conspirators, the Father of the Tunnel, and in every way one of the most important personages concerned, fell due for a fortnight of solitary confinement. He had some time ago had a violent altercation with the most odious of the parcel room attendants, and had, in the course of it, absent-mindedly handled a large knife which was lying on the parcel room counter. The attendant promptly brought a charge against him for attempted homicide, and—the word, as well as the body, of even the vilest German being sacrosanct when brought into collision with those of prisoners-of-war—Gray was in due course brought up before a court-martial. It says something for his judges on this occasion that they did not give him more than a fortnight, which in reality amounted to acquittal. There existed tribunals which would have given him six months of the best without the slightest twinge of conscience, or—more melancholy still—without the thought of having been in the least unjust. This was but an instance of the perversions of all the accepted canons of fair play which frequently occurred; fortunately for Gray and the tunnel, it was a mild sample. So the Munshi languished and knew nothing of what was passing in the tunnel, except from guarded scraps of Hindostani spoken to him in an even voice from the window of the camp adjutant's room, immediately above his cell.

Finally, Tim and his young woman made their long deliberated effort and were caught most unluckily at the main gate, thereby throwing the camp officials and Niemeyer in particular into a most undesirable mood of added watchfulness. Everything had gone according to plan up to a point—the Kommandantur staircase had again been made use of, and a most seductive little flapper typist had tripped his unassuming way unchallenged through the gate. Tim himself, dressed in a German private's uniform (but otherwise unmistakably Tim), had attempted to follow suit; but he was unable to avoid his doom in the shape of one too curious and too intelligent pair of eyes at the guard-room window. Their owner recognised him as an English officer and promptly gave the alarm. Result, the usual Tim débacle, and the work of months once again nullified. The pair were marched off to the cells under escort amidst sympathetic expressions from every side. Even Ulrich, the German officer of B Kaserne, was loud in his admiration of the disguises used; 'he had of course suspected something was up for months.' Of course.

Lieutenant Lincke, the officer who had succeeded the pot-bellied Gröner in charge of A Kaserne, a pharmacist by trade and the personification of pompous absurdity, seized the opportunity to show his ignorance of the English and his unsuitability for his post by intimating that the female disguise had been culled from the theatrical wardrobe allowed us on parole. Once again, and in accordance with cherished tradition, war had to be waged on the parole question, and the artificially good relations which were being promoted in the interests of the tunnel were temporarily suspended until Lincke could be induced to retract his entirely inexcusable inference.

It must be explained that the whole of the theatrical wardrobe, both for male and female parts, was kept strictly apart under lock and key and under the supervision of a particular officer. It had always been a strict injunction of each successive senior British officer that on no account was there to be any tampering with these clothes for the purposes of escape, and that any infringement of this order would be looked upon as a breaking of parole. This unwritten, but none the less thoroughly understood, reservation was as clear as it was necessary in the interests of that large section of the community which relied on the periodical "shows"—whether as performers or spectators—for their principal means of relief from the *ennui* of prison existence. The disguise of Tim's accomplice had, as a matter of fact, been smuggled in from the town at a considerable expenditure in German money and British kind.

But Lincke, having been, till within the last year, a

German pharmacist in a small way of business, had about as much idea of British (not to say German) military honour as he had of field operations. His training had consisted of three or four months in a Reserve of Officers Training Battalion, and he came out of it vibrant with the glory of two things—the German military system, and himself as reflecting a modest proportion of that glory. He was perfectly genial, self-satisfied, and common. On *appel* he insisted on believing that he was dealing with a company of recruits on parade, and the long, shuffling, indifferent rows of British officers winced or laughed at his antics, according to the state of their nerves. He used to begin operations by a salute with the top half of his person inclined almost at right angles with the ground ; some of the lighter spirits used to go one better and execute a complete *salaam*, and this, of course, made him querulous. He would recall to the senior officer on parade the great day when he and his brother officer-aspirants stood poker stiff at attention under inspection by one of the very biggest of the German Generals. "Scarcely a *pickelhaube* moved." That was his triumph—scarcely a *pickelhaube* had moved. And so why could not now the British officers do likewise, instead of appearing on parade in dirty uniforms and without caps and saluting so raggedly ? Oh it was too bad.

He was of course a complete nonentity and disregarded alike by Niemeyer and the British, as well as by his non-commissioned officers. But even nonentities exercise awkward powers if placed in positions where they should not be, and Lincke, for all his mildness, was about as troublesome to deal with as a Junker of the real Prussian school. His pharmaceutical soul and his hopeless inability to understand the British point of view made him in fact a serious thorn in the flesh, as was evidenced in the wardrobe incident.

Ultimately he crashed badly. He was in the habit of paying frequent visits to the tin room, nominally to inspect, actually to satisfy his craving for the sight of our English delicacies. He was insatiably inquisitive, as well as greedy, and used to spend hours together down in the cellars, questioning officers as to the contents and origin of particular tins. Finally there became reason to suspect him of something rather more serious than mere curiosity; a trap was set, and he was marked down by three witnesses in the act of abstracting tins from one of the shelves and putting them hurriedly in his pocket.

This gave us a most valuable handle, for even at Holzminden the German officers had never stolen our tins from our own tin room, or if they had, had not been such fools as to be caught doing so. In due course, and at a seasonable moment, the card was played, the written statement of the witnesses handed in, and an explanation asked for. Niemeyer took a day or two before he replied—what passed between himself and the luckless Lincke in the interval we could only guess—and then explained that it was in the regulations for German officers at any time to take tins out of the tin room in order personally to examine them for contraband articles.

The senior British officer politely noted this explanation and asked leave to refer the question to the *Kriegsministerium* for a ruling. Lincke, meanwhile, was relieved of his post. It was one of the few occasions (besides the tunnel) upon which we ever succeeded in getting really up on them.

The capture of Tim caused gloomy anticipation of a search and with it the discovery of the attempted hole in Room 34, and thereby, as a natural corollary, of the tunnel itself. In the second week of July—with three yards or so further to go before an exit could be made behind the beans, with the prospect of a search imminent at any moment, and with the added danger of an early harvest to spur their efforts—the working-party began to make their final arrangements. A week—possibly ten days—hence, and the thing would be put to the proof for better or worse.

There were thirteen of them: Lieutenants Mardock and Lawrence of the Royal Naval Air Service, Captain Gray, Lieutenant Butler, Captain Langren, Lieutenant Wainwright, R.N., Lieutenant Macleod, Captain Bain, Captain Kennard, Lieutenant Robertson, Lieutenant Clouston, Lieutenant Morris, Lieutenant Paddison. They voted for priority of station. After the working-party proper, places were allotted to Lieutenant-Colonel Rathborne, the senior officer of the camp, Lieutenant Bousfield, whose share in a previous attempt has been narrated earlier, and Captain Lyon of the Australians, who was to travel with Bousfield.

Then came a supplementary working-party of six, who, though not actually employed in the digging of the tunnel, had contributed valuable assistance in scouting-out and had made themselves generally useful in helping to dig the holes inside the actual building.

It was arranged that the original working-party should have a clear hour's start, and that another hour should intervene between the last man out of the supplementary working-party and "the ruck."

"The ruck"—or, in other words, anyone else who wanted to go—had by now assumed alarming dimensions. There were some sixty names on the official list handed to me as Camp Adjutant on the day preceding the escape. The list had been arranged in order of priority of exit, and to prevent heart-burnings—as well as to promote the maximum of secrecy—it was arranged that those on the list should only be warned in the first instance *after* the evening *appel* on the night of the actual escape. Moreover, no one was to be told his place but only that he was to lie in bed fully dressed until he was actually warned to go, upon which he was to get up at once and repair to the rendezvous on the attic floor. This was a very wise precaution. It excluded the possibility of anyone in A Kaserne getting wind of the intention to flit and then endeavouring to get into the other barrack for the night and so endangering the success of the enterprise. It also precluded the risk of excessive human circulation in the corridors, the only people authorised to move about in the corridors being myself, Lieutenant Grieve, who was selected as traffic controller, one or two look-out men, and each escaper as, in his proper turn, he left his bed to pass to the tunnel.

The orderlies had been thoroughly warned, and those of them who had volunteered to help fully understood their duties. One was to receive officers one by one on the other side of the hole in the attic room and was to signal the next man to come through when the coast was clear. Another was to guide officers to the tunnel entrance down the staircase and through the planks, and two more were to be on duty at the actual tunnel entrance. Traffic was to be carefully controlled.

Not more than two officers were to be allowed inside the orderlies' quarters at a time. If there was a hitch, Lieutenant Grieve, on the far side of the attic hole, was to be immediately warned. On discovery all the orderlies were to pretend complete ignorance of the whole business.

This last goes without saying. Just as the loyal co-operation of the orderlies was essential to success, so it was imperative that none of them should be implicated. They had all been offered a starting-place if they cared to accept one, but none of them did. The long expected, almost despaired of, head-for-head exchange had at last been arranged at the Hague, and the agreement was now only awaiting ratification. The fact that privates had been up till now excluded from the terms of the exchange had of course been very severely criticised, and it was not until later realised that the arrangements for a general head-for-head repatriation had been frustrated entirely from the German side. But the rule of "women and children first"—as our orderlies, half good naturedly, half cynically, and with that wonderful instinct for the epigrammatic which characterises the British soldier, had summarised the situation—was now obsolete. To have imperilled their chances of exchange by taking a long risk at this stage of their captivity (nearly all of them were 1914 prisoners) would have been very unwise, even had they been as well equipped as the officers as regards disguise, money, reserves of food, and general experience. Moreover, the penalties for attempted escape were for private soldiers infinitely more severe than they were for officers. They would have certainly been sent back to one of the men's

Lagers, and their previous experiences reminded them that any officers' *Lager*—even Holzminden—was considerably better than the former's best. And there were always the coal and salt mines to be taken into calculation. So they stayed behind, and their share in the night's work amply crowned their long record of ungrudged service and devotion to the cause.

During the last few days, when it was generally known that at any moment the cat might jump and it became a question of concealing "zero" day from your own side, the tension was positively painful. With the best will in the world, the injunctions of the senior British officer came to be overlooked. Even the senior British officer himself was not innocent in this respect. Small parties clustered at the ends of corridors or roamed disconsolately round and round the camp, discussing the eternal question, *When?* Civilian disguises, maps, and packs were brought out from their hiding-places and set ready for the road. More risks of detection were run during this period in a day than had been run before in a whole month. Maps were studied. An unwise and rather insubordinate eleventh-hour attempt on the part of one or two of the more desperate characters in Kaserne A to effect a transfer of rooms to Kaserne B was fortunately quashed. The senior British officer, who was somewhat square-rigged in shape, was given a trial run down the tunnel to see if he could manage it. It took him an hour to get back!

Walks had been allowed again as a consequence of the "lifting" of the reprisals, and most of the intending starters availed themselves of this opportunity to get into good marching trim. Fit as they were in consequence of the strenuous work down below, they felt the need of using every available opportunity for a good heel-and-toe movement over a stretch of unconfined ground. The Holland border was 120 kilometres away and would not easily be reached by those who had let their walking muscles lie too long dormant. In addition, it was pleasant to get away for a space from the strained atmosphere of the enclosure and the tremendous secret of the camp, and without constraint to think and talk for a little of other things. In high midsummer the plain in which we walked was only less lovely than it had been in the spring. As then the trees, so now the young crops invited us to build up a new calendar in terms of growing things. We may not have felt the need perhaps, in the years gone by, to pay due note to the wonderful kaleidoscope. Now the very circumscription of her lecturing hours made Nature's lessons the more highly prized.

Sometimes, when the weather was warm and the Feldwebel in charge sufficiently lazy and complacent, we bathed in the Weser—clandestinely, for river bathing was not allowed by the municipal authorities. Then for a glorious half-hour the river would be alive with the nude bodies of a hundred happy men. It was established at these bathes that the river was easily fordable at one point. In our parole cards there was nothing down to tell us not to *notice* things. And the river lay between the camp and Holland.

At the last moment another painful incident occurred. It became known that a certain desperate party in A Kaserne were proposing to anticipate the tunnel, and the increased restrictions which its discovery would be bound to create, by some wild-cat scheme of their own. It appeared to be their intention to fuse the lights all over the building and make a bid to get over the wire in the darkness and confusion thus created. There was also going to be employed a "blind" in the shape of a large dummy figure dropped from a window at the opposite end of the building to that at which the actual attempt was to be made. The scheme in ordinary circumstances would have been worth trying and was a courageous one. But at this juncture of affairs, when the work of nine months was on the verge of bearing fruit, and when the one thing needed was to lull the suspicions of the authorities, it was foolish and selfish. To make matters worse, the participants had received the unofficial support of the senior officer in the building.

The senior British officer in the camp, however, took a very different line. He had the ringleader up and put the argument fairly and forcibly before him. He sympathised, of course, but—there was a train already in the tunnel. The line was not quite clear for it yet, but would be shortly, and it must be let through first. It was very important not to have a collision at this moment, and the advent of another train might spell disaster. He must definitely forbid any prior attempt.

But for the above-mentioned ringleader, the tunnel would have been essayed a night earlier than it actually was. On the doors of the houses being locked at nightfall on the 23rd July, it was found that the fellow was in B Kaserne. He had got wind of it somehow and was determined to be in at the death. The only course was to cancel the operation for the night and induce this officer to realise that he had made a mistake and explain his appearance in the wrong house to the Feldwebel as best he could. Elaborate measures were also taken to put him off the scent for the ensuing night. Disciplinary methods were really useless with this type; besides, the senior officer was too closely occupied in the final arrangements of his own intricate disguise—he was intending to travel by train in broad daylight and not as a thief in the night—to feel any inclination for taking any further steps with this refractory individual.

Such difficulties may sound petty, perhaps, and inconsistent with the spirit of comradeship. But it was not in human nature to risk the fruits of eight months' incessant labour to benefit the crowd. Nerves were badly on edge, and the wonder really is that this particular intruder was let off as lightly as he was.

CHAPTER IX

THE ESCAPE AND THE SEQUEL

THE reader will excuse if at this point in the story the first person pronoun figures rather prominently. I was myself at this time the Adjutant of the camp, and, as such, had been fairly thoroughly coached how things were to be done. I was very glad to have the opportunity of contributing, in however modest a degree, to the success of the plot. The glorious nature of the adventure came home to me at last, and I experienced some rather severe eleventh-hour twinges of regret that I had not availed myself more fully of any chances that I might have had of actually participating. There had been times of late when I had almost given up the tunnel. There had seemed to be no end to the difficulties and obstacles in completing it. Added to which, the ordinary routine duties of Adjutant had kept me too fully occupied to acquire the proper escaper's atmosphere and spend long hours over preparing maps and packs and securing the necessary money and disguise. Frankly, I had been a little sceptical.

Later on, in another camp, where there was full latitude to mature one's scheme and the Germans interfered hardly at all with one's daily doings, I experienced the complete escape fever. But that is another story.

The actual night of the escape was the 24th July.

I was warned just before evening *appel*, at 6 o'clock, that if B house harboured no aliens that night, the escape would take place. I got hold of Grieve during the evening and we held a long confabulation as to how the policing had best be done. It was arranged that I should do all the warning and escort people to the rendezvous in the attic, and that he should do the actual controlling and keep in communication with the orderlies. The evening passed away and I don't think anybody outside the working-party was aware that anything was actually in the wind.

The doors in B house were safely locked at 9.0 p.m. without a single intruder from A house. Several people had been keenly on the watch to see to this point. We went off quietly to our respective rooms to have our names called.

After the Feldwebel and his minions had finally left the building, there was still another hour or so to wait before the coast was clear for action. A German sentry used to come round some time after 10 o'clock to close all the windows in the corridors and incidentally remove anything that he saw to his liking which might be lying about. Until he had gone it would be unsafe to have any undue movement, and only the cutting-out man— i.e. the first officer to go through the tunnel—and the two next on the list would go down to the chamber before he was well clear.

During this period of waiting the senior British officer paid me a visit in his dressing-gown and said good-bye. I wished him good luck. We had worked together for two months or more and had discussed the tunnel and his particular plan to escape countless times. He had a very good disguise and, without wishing to disparage his features, they were—with the aid of glasses—wonderfully Teutonic. He was, so far as I knew, the only one who was proposing to travel all the way to the frontier by train, and with his excellent knowledge of German and forged papers he looked to have a very good chance.

I sat in my room until the outside door had slammed behind the German sentry and I knew the working-party would have already begun making their way through the tunnel for the last time. Then I began going round the rooms and warning personally every man on the list. They were to get their kit ready and get into bed fully dressed and then wait until they were called. There was to be no movement in the corridors of any sort. For all the secrecy that had been attempted, they were most of them more than half expecting the long-deferred call. Probably someone had seen a member of the working-party in his disguise and had passed on the information. A few of them wanted to know where they were in the list, but I told them that they were not to know and had only to obey orders. Everyone would have to come upstairs in his socks, carrying his boots in his hand. After I had completed the task of warning everybody I went up to see Grieve. It was now past half-past eleven. He told me that the working-party were all well away already and that the thing was going well.

The hour's law for the working-party was strictly adhered to, and at 12.30 the supplementary working-party began to go through. They, too, were all through by about 1.15.

At 1.10 or thereabouts I began my duties of assembling those on the waiting list. Two or three passed through all right, and then the orderly on the orderlies' side of the attic hole passed the word back that there was a hitch. He would let Grieve know when it was all clear again.

The next man due to go through had overweighted himself and his pack to such an extent that the delay proved perhaps a blessing in disguise. If we had let him go through as he was, he would probably have stuck in the tunnel, would most certainly not have forded the Weser, and could, in any case, not have marched for more than three days. We sent him back with some stern advice to remove a dozen tins or so from his pack, discard his stick, and take off his hobnailed boots which had made an infernal clatter in the passage. A few more such performers and the secret would be out!

No news came through from the tunnel, so I decided to turn in for an hour or so, and Grieve arranged for a message to be sent to me if the coast was clear before that time.

I took a turn up and down the corridors before I lay down. There were the sentries outside walking up and down, with their chins sunk on their breasts and their rifles slung on their backs, wonderfully as usual. It was odd to think that within a hundred yards our fellows were wriggling away through the rye. Clearly nothing had been suspected so far. It was a calm night and fairly dark.

I lay down knowing that there would be heaps of work to do the next day, whatever happened, and that I should want my wits about me. But I could not sleep, and at about 2.30 I went upstairs to see Grieve again. He reported there was no change in the position.

We tried to get an answer from the orderlies' quarters, but there was no reply. It was rather baffling. At 3 o'clock we held a council of war with Captain Sharp, who was one of those due to go through early in the list, and we agreed—although it was against the instructions given us, which had been that the orderlies should alone be responsible for letting anyone through the attic hole—that Sharp should go through to reconnoitre. He did so, and came back in about a quarter of an hour's time to report that no one was about, and that the tunnel was empty[1].

It was rather a nasty moment. We had a sudden new suspicion of insecurity and a feeling that valuable time might have been lost. It now wanted about two hours to dawn, and so far we reckoned that only 24 were out of the camp. It did not look very promising for most of the waiting list.

In the absence of the orderlies—we hardly felt justified in giving them further orders—we sent through the next five officers on the waiting list, headed by Sharp, allowing five minutes between each. They did not return, so we concluded that the tunnel was still clear and that they had got away, thus bringing the total number to 29. About half a dozen more had followed at regular intervals, and it was getting on for half-past four, when the last—Captain Gardiner of the A.I.F.—came back to report that the tunnel was blocked and passage impossible. According to his report the tunnel was reverberating with groans, curses, and expressions of encouragement. Someone apparently was stuck in front and was urging

[1] It was never found out exactly what caused the check and I do not think it ever will be.

those behind him to get back in order to let him out. Those behind, on the other hand, like the Tuscans in the famous Lay, were crying "Forward" in no uncertain tones, and urging him to get out and on with it. It had clearly become a hopeless impasse. It seemed best, therefore, at this juncture to call a halt and clear the course before daylight, so as to defer the chance of discovery till the last possible moment. Recommendations were therefore passed along to evacuate the tunnel.

But here arose another difficulty. Those now labouring in the tunnel were not used to its ways. It was hard enough to wriggle along in a forward direction, but withdrawal, with a heavy pack in tow, was an even more strenuous proposition. It will be remembered that the working-party, with muscles attuned by long practice, had experienced the utmost difficulty in pulling out the sacks of earth when the rope method broke down. And to get the packs out was an absolute necessity, for otherwise there would be a complete block both before and behind, which would result in the foremost unfortunates being entombed until the tunnel was discovered and they were dug out.

The situation called for desperate measures, and fortunately the right man was at hand. A New Zealand officer called Garland, who was high up on the waiting list, came up to the rendezvous to prospect. He happened to be about as strong physically as any other two officers in the camp, and possessed the biceps of a Hercules. He at once volunteered to go down and try to pull out the rear-most man.

After about half an hour he succeeded in doing so, and the two collaborators in this severe physical exercise crawled back through the attic hole completely exhausted and dripping with sweat.

There still remained four men stuck in the tunnel, it was already getting light, and in an hour and a half —at 6 a.m.—a German N.C.O. was due to open the outside door and call the orderlies. It was essential, therefore, to get everyone back into the building before that time. If the alarm of the escape was not raised before 9 o'clock *appel*, the 29 fugitives now at large would have all the better opportunity of making cover some distance away from the camp before they lay up for their first day out.

An hour past a look-out from an upper window at the end of one of the corridors had reported that two figures had been seen in the dim half light of the dawn making off through the rye field. It was guessed that these would probably be the last pair out before the accident had happened in the tunnel which had barred further passage. If this couple could gain the Duke of Brunswick's hunting woods—some three miles distant —before the hue and cry was out, they could lie up snugly and safely, and their predecessors would be in all the better plight.

The work of extracting the remaining four went on slowly and laboriously, and by a quarter to six two more mudstained objects had been salved and had been sent back, cursing bitterly, to their rooms to get rid of their mud and cover their traces. It appeared that the tunnel had caved in about five-sixths of the way up—at the bottom of the slope up to the final exit. Stones loosened in the traffic had found their way to this—the lowest point in the whole tunnel, and were blocking further progress. A landslip on the most modest scale would be quite enough to block up the tiny hole.

There was now nothing left to do. The two officers still in the tunnel with the volunteers assisting them to get out would have to be left to take their chance. Everybody else went back to their rooms and to bed, hugging themselves in anticipation of the 9 o'clock *appel*, and the fireworks which would inevitably ensue when the Feldwebel of B house reported with a rueful countenance that according to his reckoning there "failed" (*fehlen*) no less than twenty-nine *Herren*.

This hope was, however, frustrated, and the bubble burst two hours too soon. The two last men in the tunnel were eventually retrieved, and emerged from the plank entrance with their rescuers to find the door at the orderlies' entrance open. The under-officer had duly called the orderlies some twenty minutes previously and had gone away suspecting nothing. Their obvious course was to obey instructions and go back to their house by the same way as they had come. But for some reason they failed to do so and ran out very foolishly into the cookhouse in the enclosure, where they met Niemeyer out for an inopportune early morning stroll. Their salvage party meanwhile had gone back by the proper way.

In ten minutes the whole of the camp staff had appeared on the scene. The two officers, of course, refused to say anything or to explain their muddy condition. Even then Niemeyer failed to tumble to what had actually occurred. But a few minutes later an excited farmer appeared at the postern gate and led the whole party to where, amid the trampled rye in which a dozen different tracks were visible from the camp windows, a gaping hole brought recognition and late wisdom to Milwaukee Bill.

"*So, ein Tunnel.*"

Tunnel. The same dangerous word, common to either language, which had been whispered for so long by the one side, now ran like electricity through the ranks of the other.

The next question from Niemeyer's point of view was, how many? The fat Feldwebel went off and counted an expectant house. He found everybody unusually wide awake and good humoured for that hour of the morning. The fat Feldwebel was himself thoroughly amused by the eventful happenings since his last appearance in the house, and he merely chortled good-humouredly as name after name elicited no response. He returned to the rye field to report to Niemeyer an absentee list of 26. In his excitement he had forgotten to count the "Munshi's" room, from which all three occupants had flitted.

Then came the real moment. Niemeyer's jaw dropped, his moustachios for a brief instant lost their twirl, his solid stomach swelled less impressively against his overcoat. Just for a moment he became grey and looked very old. But only for a moment. The sound of laughter in the upper corridor windows floated down to him and roused action and the devil in him forthwith. As an initial measure he put all the windows at that end of the building out of bounds and told his sentries to fire at once if a face appeared. Then he had the outer doors of both houses locked. Then he placed a sentry over the tunnel head and stalked away to the Kom-

mandantur to ring up the Company Captain in Holzminden, inform the police, report events to Corps
Headquarters at Hanover, and issue emergency orders
"for the safety of the camp."

These were posted up in both houses and caused
considerable amusement. Briefly, they permitted the
officers remaining in the camp to eat, sleep, and breathe,
but that was about all. "No one," so ran the order,
"when inside the building was to move from his own
room. Conversation with other officers in the corridors
or by the notice boards was forbidden. Officers were
not allowed to stand about at the doors of the buildings.
No officer belonging to one house might enter the
other. Officers were not to walk about in groups of
more than two." And so on.

Of course we had amply expected all this. Indeed,
there was ground for congratulation that things had
panned out up to the present without murder being
done. Stringent orders had been issued that, in the event
of the escape only being discovered at the 9 o'clock *appel*,
there was to be no laughter or demonstration calculated
to aggravate. Months before, the more serious-minded
had discussed the prospects of someone being shot in
the Commandant's first wild ebullition of fury and
baffled rage at the defeat of all his precautions. It was
one advantage of the premature discovery of the escape
that what shooting was ordered was confined to the
windows.

Twenty-nine. The magic number flitted from mouth
to mouth and was shouted across from B house to A,
who cheered heartily on hearing the figure. It was indeed a good number and constituted an easy record for

Germany, if not for all time. *Neun und zwanzig.* Long
ere now it had permeated to the town, and the road outside the camp was strangely peopled with unusual
figures of both sexes and all ages, anxious to view the
scene of the occurrence, and most of them no doubt
vastly pleased at the discomfiture of the notorious bully,
Hauptmann Niemeyer. Always the camp had been the
diversion of a Sunday evening stroll for the burghers
of Holzminden; now we played daily to crowded
houses, until the Commandant, in his exasperation, put
the confines of the camp out of bounds to civilians.
Those who had been stuck in the hours of the dawn
exchanged experiences and friendly recrimination. Personal disappointment was merged in the general triumph.
For triumph it was. Twenty-nine loose in Germany.
Twenty-nine. He would have been a bold man who
would have breathed that number in Niemeyer's hearing.

The sentries grinned as they echoed it. Kasten, the
fat old Feldwebel, laughed as he notched it on the next
(mid-day) *appel.* And Niemeyer tried to digest it.

He was not very successful. We were let out of the
barracks after mid-day. No attempt was naturally made
to fall in with the newly posted camp regulations, and
serious collisions with Niemeyer, as soon as he came
abroad, were inevitable. There was at the bottom of
everybody's mind a feeling that the time had at last
come to be rid of him, that now the star of the Great
Twin Brethren might at last wane and the wrath from
Hanover or Berlin descend on the discredited favourite
for being unable either to keep his gaol-birds at home or
to keep order in his own house. But bloodshed was to be

avoided. It was a difficult policy, to annoy by pinpricks, to goad an already maddened creature, but to keep, as a community, within the law. But it was the right policy, and one which commended itself to the new senior British officer, Colonel Stokes Roberts, who succeeded to the position vacated by Colonel Rathborne, now well on his way to freedom.

Accordingly the red rag was discreetly held out, and Niemeyer retained just enough self-control not to draw and flourish a revolver. All the available cells were filled within the first few hours with candidates for three days' arrest. Their crimes were imaginary and were not stated. They might have failed to salute at 40 paces, they might have laughed, they might merely have happened to be standing somewhere in Niemeyer's path. It did not matter. They had certainly all broken the latest camp regulations.

All the orderlies were taken off duty and set to dig up the tunnel. The tin rooms and parcel rooms were closed until further notice. I myself, whose complicity with the plot was highly suspected, was removed from my own room and bundled unceremoniously into one of the large rooms on the top floor of A house. The windows of the cells were barricaded up and made quite dark by day and the lights in them were kept on all night. Every German in the camp personnel was put on to sentry duty and sentries paraded the passages three times in the night. The use of the bath room attendant for this purpose precluded baths. In a word we were "strafed," and the camp knew once more the open warfare which had prevailed for the first unforgettable month of its existence.

Orderlies digging out the tunnel between Kaserne B and the outer wall.

The inconveniences of such a state of affairs were lightly borne, and even relished, by the large majority. The Tunnellers had scored too heavily for us to mind doing scapegoat for them. It was a pleasant thought that all twenty-nine were still abroad, and that there was a reasonable certainty of a fair proportion of them getting over and putting a stop to Niemeyer's run of atrocious good luck in the matter of escapes. Apart from the hue and cry which had already been raised through the North German press, the fugitives had everything in their favour. They had had months to deliberate on their route and travelling tactics; their packs had been stocked at leisure so as to combine the maximum of nutrition with the minimum of weight; their civilian disguises were adequate for their purpose. Most of them were going to trust to their legs to carry them over the border and would be only night birds of passage, lying up during the day. But Colonel Rathborne possessed a knowledge of German and a superb civilian suit, over which he had put pyjamas in going through the tunnel, and which would be able to set casual interference blandly at defiance. He was walking due south to Göttingen and was there going to entrain for Aachen *viâ* Cassel and Frankfurt. If all went well with him and his forged passport passed muster, he would be over the frontier in under three days. And later, when six days had gone by and he had not returned, the camp knew that the spell had been broken and that an Englishman was over from Holzminden. But we said nothing to the Germans.

However, before six days had passed a good number of the twenty-nine had already been rounded up and brought back to camp. As they were kept in the strictest isolation, it was only possible to hear their stories by bribing the cell attendants to bring written messages from them. If bribes failed, the message was concealed somehow in their trays of food. Every officer in detention cell had to have a friend to feed him—i.e. cook his food and see that it was delivered to him ; otherwise he existed in semi-starvation on the German ration. It was the usual thing, preparatory to an attempt to escape, to arrange for your feeding arrangements in "jug" ; and the penalty of recapture was shared to the full by the luckless partner, who thus had double work.

Sharp and Luscombe were the first pair back, as they had been the last pair away. They had had two days and a night out and had been caught passing through a village at night about 15 miles down the Weser. Sharp reported that at his search on being brought back to the camp, Niemeyer had vented his spleen on him by picking a valuable gold watch to pieces with his pocket knife, and by giving instructions for his civilian clothes (which included a brand new coat from England) to be ripped to ribbons. Every day brought in some fresh recapture, and, the cell accommodation being completely inadequate to cope with the numerous criminals, the town gaol was drawn upon to afford relief.

It was a sad blow to the camp when some of the foremost spirits in the adventure—Mardock, Lawrence, Butler, and Langren—were brought back after being out about ten days. Butler had stolen a bicycle and was caught on it while passing through a village. The others had been taken in the vicinity of the Ems. All these separate captures used to be described at length and with appropriate embellishments in the Hanoverian press. Thus in one organ it was stated that the refugees were all wearing British uniform; another had it that British naval uniform was the mode, with the buttons altered; yet another explained that the prisoners had escaped in civilian disguise procured from British friends outside the camp. To be sure, we had British friends outside the camp—what prisoner-of-war did not? But one could imagine the burghers of Hanover reading this sort of stuff and commenting on the lax policy of the Government towards enemy aliens!

A detective from Berlin had arrived shortly after the escape and displayed the usual aptitude of his species in examining the tunnel. Several hours elapsed before he found the door in the partition. This was all in Niemeyer's favour, since a mere Commandant, a layman in the science of crime, could not reasonably have been expected to guess the secret which had temporarily baffled the expert. Such acuteness would have been unseemly and unprofessional. The detective took a large number of photographs[1] and made a large number of notes, and the two parted on the best of terms. When Niemeyer had bowed the important visitor off the premises, he turned his attention once more to the safe keeping of the British officers still remaining under his wing.

For several days he achieved a crescendo of fury and malevolence and maintained all the outward characteristics of a mad bull. Unfortunately he had not in any way fallen from grace. A staff officer from Hanover specially sent down to examine the affair was, to

[1] Three of these are reproduced in this book.

our disappointment, an apparently appreciative witness of his behaviour. We had calculated that von Hänisch would by now have discovered a flaw in his chosen instrument, and that the attitude of the chief might be seen to be reflected in his subordinates. But we were out of our reckoning. The captain from Hanover used even to accompany Niemeyer in his periodical incursions into the camp precincts and stand stolidly by while the latter blackguarded every Englishman within reach or hearing.

Possibly Niemeyer had got ideas from reading Don Quixote on his dull evenings. One of his favourite amusements during this period was to make fierce onslaughts with his stick on the washing hanging out to dry on the wire fence between the two main buildings. He would lunge at some unoffending under-garment, spit it, brandish it violently in the air, and then trample on it. It was against the regulations for washing to be hung on the wire, and the Commandant sacrificed his personal dignity to see that these regulations were unflinchingly obeyed.

His behaviour towards the orderlies was a delightful contrast. Usually domineering and foul-mouthed towards them beyond the ordinary, he was now honey-tongued good fellowship itself. The orderlies were all employed digging up the tunnel; and Niemeyer used to stand by them for hours at a time, asking the men questions about their homes in England, their wives and children, and generally trying to put himself on the best possible terms with them.

Niemeyer was looking desperately hard for a scape-goat. It is to be remembered that no one had been caught actually *in* the tunnel, and every officer recaptured stoutly refused to say how he had got out. There was no tangible evidence of any conspiracy. Consequently unless an admission of complicity was wrung from one of the orderlies, the charge of doing damage to German property, levelled against a number of unconvicted and unconvictable persons, would lose weight, however circumstantial the evidence; and it was punishment to the hilt which the Commandant, in his wounded pride, yearned after. But his clumsy overtures took in nobody. The men knew that he was trying his hardest to pump them and gave nothing away.

CHAPTER X

CLOSING INCIDENTS

NIEMEYER had often, in more peaceful days, jocularly remarked that the conduct of the British officers was making him an old man before his time. Such of us as in these days were brought face to face with him began to get a comfortable feeling that this indeed was the case. He was reported to be 62; and by this time he was looking every day of it.

The actual *casus belli* on which the senior British officer decided to force the issue was the treatment, on the day after the escape, of an R.F.C. officer called Phelan. This officer had on his way down to the cells been brutally kicked by a sentry under the approving eye of a particularly odious Feldwebel of the best Prussian pattern surnamed Klausen, and known familiarly as "Dog Face." The act had been witnessed by at least six British officers and the evidence duly taken down. The senior British officer therefore gave the Phelan incident pride of place in a summary sent to Niemeyer of various individual and collective injustices visited on the members of the camp since the discovery of the tunnel, and added a curt ultimatum that unless these grievances were promptly redressed he would be unable to be responsible for the further conduct of the British officers.

This was an extreme step and had never, even in this turbulent camp, been employed before. For the senior

British officer to disclaim authority over his own brother-officers implied, legally speaking, that he regarded the conditions of imprisonment as too monstrous to be covered by the accepted rules of the Hague Convention, and that in fact he looked upon the Commandant not as his sentinel in an honourable captivity under the rules of war, but as his gaoler in a common gaol, where international conventions did not apply. Once this attitude was taken up, the ordinary courtesies of military etiquette would have to be abandoned, salutes not offered, passive resistance everywhere adopted. Uniformity of conduct would be an absolute essential, and elaborate precautions were taken to warn the camp by word of mouth—paper would have been too dangerous—exactly what procedure was to be followed if the order went forth that diplomatic relations had been broken off with the Huns.

The Adjutant's position in those stormy days was an onerous one. It was the essence of the whole British policy that the senior officer's orders should be carried out to the letter. Due allowance had also to be made for the incalculable perversity of the " half per cent " to whom reference has already been made. Both of these duties fell to the Adjutant of the camp working through the Adjutants of the houses. Written instructions were impossible on account of the risk. It was necessary to warn personally every one of the 500 odd officers in the camp and to explain when, and if necessary why, action was to be taken in accordance with "scheme of resistance A or B."

No reply was received to the ultimatum, and it was decided therefore to put into execution a general scheme of passive resistance. On the morning after the expiry of the ultimatum the entire camp shuffled late and listlessly on to 9 o'clock *appel*, wearing, for the most part, cardigan jackets instead of tunics, and innocent of all headgear. When the German officers appeared, no one saluted or paid the slightest attention to them. Ulrich hesitated, grasped the situation, and went straight back to the Kommandantur to report. He returned with a message from the Commandant to the senior British officer that if he could arrange for an orderly *appel* in an hour's time he (the Commandant) would be glad to discuss matters and examine the list of grievances submitted.

So far, so good. The word was circulated for a perfect *appel* at 10 a.m. But at 10 o'clock, after the conclusion of an *appel* which, for correctness of dress and demeanour, would have satisfied the soul even of the late lamented Lincke, Niemeyer strode on to the middle of the parade ground and disillusioned us :

" Well, yentlemen," he bawled out, " You have broken the camp regulations, so you must be punished. There will be no sport for three days."

The camp was too flabbergasted even to boo or groan. We had trusted him and paid the obvious penalty. The whole incident was typically Prussian.

Colonel Stokes Roberts did the only possible thing under the circumstances and countered with an order for another passive resistance *appel* at 5 o'clock. Once again tunics and caps were discarded and the long rows of ragamuffins stood listlessly awaiting the pleasure of their gaolers to come and count them. There was likely to be trouble this time, for the authorities would be forewarned, and it was noticed that the guard were standing paraded in front of the Kommandantur. It was just a question of how far our friend would dare to go. The action of the British was seen from the Kommandantur and the German officers did not even come on *appel*. An interpreter was sent out to order all officers to go back to their houses. As we trailed off the parade ground Niemeyer appeared at the head of about a dozen sentries with bayonets fixed and roared to us to get into our houses "right away." As there was only one door in each house this was an impossible feat, and the disreputable crowd merely grinned at the sheepish sentries and the Commandant fulminating from one barrack to another. The British acted creditably up to their allotted part of brainless, dejected criminals, and there was no demonstration or provocative action as we gradually melted away into our respective barracks.

One officer, however, who had on board rather more than was good for him, did his best to promote bloodshed. He dropped a large faggot from an upper window in B Kaserne which missed Niemeyer by inches. Beside himself with rage, the Commandant ordered the nearest sentry to fire, indicating the only officer then within sight, a lame flying officer, as the target. The man, who was really not to be blamed, fired up the staircase up which the officer was making all haste to retreat, missed him by a few inches, and splintered a window. Then the doors were closed and we breathed again.

The counter-charge of mutiny was brought by Niemeyer, when in company with the Hanover staff captain he interviewed Colonel Stokes Roberts that evening. The camp had publicly mutinied, and the mutiny would have to be made the subject of a special report. The senior British officer desired nothing better. A special report, he suggested, might eventually result in bringing facts to light. He begged the Commandant's permission to forward two letters to the Dutch Legation at Berlin and to the *Kriegsministerium*, which contained point-blank accusations of misconduct against the Commandant. By German law Niemeyer was bound to forward these letters, however much he disliked their matter. It did not, however, at all follow that he would do so, and accordingly, to prevent any possibility of miscarriage, duplicate letters were smuggled out of the camp into the safe keeping of the love-sick typist with injunctions to deliver the goods. The letter to the *Kriegsministerium* asked urgently for an inspection of the camp by a responsible superior officer.

So far the campaign had proceeded satisfactorily ; the case sooner or later would be put against Niemeyer without delicacy or reserve before the supreme German military authority. Then the whole history of the camp could be bluntly narrated, the damning Black Book hauled up from its hiding-place in Room 24 of B house and presented for inspection and comment. The cards were in our hands now, if we had the opportunity of playing them. Only the tribunal must be reasonably impartial and Niemeyer must not be suffered to interpret. Too many a good chance had gone begging ere this in the camp's history, simply because the Commandant, in conducting an interview, had systematically interpreted black as white and adroitly diverted the discussion from the subject of himself. It had been an unfortunate coincidence that whenever a representative from the *Kriegsministerium* in Berlin had visited the camp either he had been unable to speak English or the senior British officer of the time had been unable to speak German. The Commandant, with his fluent knowledge of English, had invariably provided the convenient bridge and the interview had accordingly failed miserably in its object.

Until the visit from the *Kriegsministerium*, conditions remained much as before, except that we gave orderly *appels*. Our policy was to lie low and await whatever Daniel the *Kriegsministerium* should deign to send us. Niemeyer seemed determined to make what hay he could while the sun shone. His way of doing so took the form of gross personal discourtesy to the senior British officer. On the day after the letters to the Dutch Legation and German War Office had been handed in, he stalked on to *appel*, went up to Colonel Stokes Roberts, and asked him in a menacing tone if he took full responsibility for all that had been written in them. On an answer being given in the affirmative, he became violently abusive and ordered the Colonel to produce another speaker in his stead, as he would have no more to do with him. He then proceeded publicly to insult Colonel Stokes Roberts in a manner absolutely unprecedented. Colonel Roberts, after the first salute, had been standing, as was customary, at ease in the orthodox manner. Niemeyer suddenly bellowed to him to stand at attention. "I guess you'll speak to me at attention. Put your heels closer—CLOSER." It was the very last straw and made cheeks flame and ears tingle in the agony of furious humiliation.

Niemeyer persisted in his demand for another "speaker" to represent the camp, only giving away his lamentable ignorance of our military customs in even formulating the request. As a joke, the names of some of his most avowed and outspoken enemies were submitted for his approval. Prominent on this list was the name of Lieutenant Beyfus, a barrister of repute, a prisoner of three years' standing, and, on frequent occasions, an able exponent to Niemeyer on the rights of the individual in captivity. Niemeyer, whose sense of humour failed him in these days, furiously repudiated such a preposterous nomination.

"No, no," he fumed; "I will not have ze Beyfus; get me another."

We were paying for the tunnel; but every day that passed now without someone being brought back increased our hopes that it had not been dug in vain. Colonel Rathborne was by now certainly over. "Munshi" Gray, Bousfield, three others of the working-party, and four not of the working-party were still abroad; and it was a fortnight since the night of the escape. Further, the opening of the big allied offensive on August 8th put new heart into us. The first day's advance showed a great slice on our well-conned maps that looked indeed like the moving warfare for which we had, in our own far-off day, so often made preparation in vain. Also we heard on reliable authority that a Bavarian regiment moving from the Bulgarian to the Western Front had mutinied at some place quite near; and such of the more Left of the German papers as we were permitted to read were full of their proposed campaign for the autumn session of the Reichstag. It was a more healthy atmosphere altogether than in the terrible days of March only four and a half months ago.

Any suspected officers in either Kaserne received short shrift in these days, and were bundled unceremoniously from their rooms into safer quarters on the ground floor of A Kaserne, where the lower windows were never open and the flies and staleness of the atmosphere were correspondingly oppressive. Billets in this way were found for any officers who had been known to have escaped before and who were referred to feelingly by Niemeyer as "the yentlemen." These particular rooms used to be visited two or three times in a night by a Feldwebel with an electric torch, which he used to flash on the occupant of each bed in turn, thereby effectually waking everybody up. Here lay the afore-mentioned and eloquent Beyfus, whose recent arrival had prevented his obtaining a place in the tunnel scheme, but whose record made him a marked man with the authorities. Here I myself lay, after yet another enforced migration from the attic floor in A house, and in accordance—so lied[1] the official intimation—with orders from Hanover. And here also lay Leefe Robinson, V.C., whose gallant spirit Niemeyer, with subtle cruelty, had endeavoured for months past to break. That Robinson's untimely death on his return from captivity was assisted indirectly by the treatment which he received at the hands of Niemeyer no one will deny who was in a position to witness that treatment.

The handling to which Leefe Robinson was subjected was so outrageous that it was communicated to the home authorities in a concealed report (in the hollow

[1] This is possibly an injustice. I found out afterwards that my parcels contained contraband.

of a tennis racket handle) *viâ* an exchange party. Robinson had come from Freiburg in Baden, where he had made an attempt with several others to escape. "The English Richthofen"—as Niemeyer, with coarse urbanity, called him to his face—was at once singled out as the victim of a malevolent scheme of repression. He was placed in the most uncomfortable room in the camp, whereas his rank entitled him to the privileges of a small room; he was caused to answer to a special *appel* two or three times in a day; and he was forbidden under any pretext to enter Kaserne B. On the occasion of a visit from some Inspecting General, and on the pretext of all the rooms having to be cleaned up and ready for inspection by 9 o'clock *appel*, Robinson's room was entered by a Feldwebel and sentries at 7.45 a.m., and Robinson himself was forcibly pulled out of bed and the table next to the bed upset on the floor. Two hours later Niemeyer was introducing "the English Richthofen" to the august visitor with a profusion of oleaginous compliments, and four hours later Robinson was in the cells for having disobeyed camp orders. Truly most damnable and cowardly persecution.

Notwithstanding all this, the Chamber of Horrors (as the room devoted to the criminals used popularly to be known) was the scene of many a humorous incident. Restricted space caused the bed of the eloquent Beyfus to be very near the door. On the flooring just inside the door lay the mat upon which Beyfus used to stand to undress. Whenever the Germans came into the room Beyfus always contrived that the door should impinge upon some part of his person and seized the occasion to call every German within hail—the Commandant, of course, for choice—to witness the unprovoked attack upon his blushing modesty. Great effect was added when the harangue was delivered in the passage and only in shirt and slippers.

The Spanish "flu," which descended in those days in an all embracing form on the camp, brought some compensating humour. In the first place, Niemeyer got it at once and was reported, quite incorrectly, to be dying. The wish, both amongst Germans and British, was doubtless father to this rumour. Then all the orderlies got it at the same time and the officers swept and garnished for themselves. And finally, when the disease had filtered through from the orderlies and taken fair hold of the officers, every room in both barracks was filled with the groans of those who thought they were about to die. As a matter of fact not more than a dozen were at all seriously ill, and these recovered quite rapidly.

The long expected visit from the *Kriegsministerium* representative synchronised with the tail end of the outbreak and came at precisely the wrong moment.

In the first place, I was sick. It should have been my business to warn the senior British officer of the visit, and arrange for an English officer to interpret his remarks at the interview. Unfortunately, and through nobody's fault, nothing of this sort was done. Colonel Stokes Roberts was sent for at a moment's notice and had his hand forced. Niemeyer once again acted as interpreter, the blinkers were kept on throughout, and the visitor went away satisfied that the complaints made by the British had been grossly exaggerated, that Niemeyer, in spite of his reputation, was, after all, a very pleasant fellow, and that there was nothing to report on unfavourably in the conduct of the camp.

Thus the rebellion at Holzminden petered unsatisfactorily out; it had been no one's fault that the chance had come and gone untaken. But it was evident that it would not come again, and that the last final effort to remove Niemeyer had been as fruitless as the first. On the other side, the charge of general mutiny was not pressed, and legal proceedings were reserved only for those implicated in the tunnel. Gradually the sombre camp resumed its normal working. A new Adjutant succeeded to office, and I, together with other suspected criminals, was transported to a camp of more fancied security. Under the new Adjutant some form of co-operation in the general interests with the German authorities became once more possible.

His predecessor, bundled out of the camp with two other officers at two hours' notice, had the pleasure, before leaving, of firing one Parthian shot at the Commandant. The evening before, an unsigned postcard had been received from the Hague. It ran simply—"Cheeroh old bean," and was addressed to Colonel Rathborne's late mess-mate. We communicated the substance of this postcard to Niemeyer, and it was some consolation, before we shook the dust of Holzminden off our feet for ever, to see the confession of defeat written plainly in his face. Once again—and for the first time since the original discovery of the escape—speech fairly failed him.

. . . .

Events, however, were moving too rapidly now for it to be a matter of great consequence to Niemeyer even that he should have let a full-blown Lieutenant-Colonel slip through his fingers. His own hour was near to striking. As the British advance in September continued without respite and the inevitable end came ever nearer, so this disreputable old man changed his tactics accordingly. He very rarely came within the precincts of the camp; but he saw the Adjutant almost daily, and at every interview some concession or other long striven for was now readily given. He even began to prepare the ground for a *volte-face* in his Prussian creed and politics. The picture of the Kaiser vanished from the wall of his sanctum. He became the strangest and most undignified contrast to the swaggering bully who had ruled this roost so long. And finally when, on the conclusion of hostilities, the *Arbeiter und Soldaten Rat* took over the military direction of affairs in the town, he was suffered to disappear unmolested and cover his tracks as best he might. It is not known what has happened to him. Both Niemeyers figured on the Black List communicated by the Supreme Council to the German Government during or after the Peace Conference. One of them was supposed to have died. But it does not really very much matter. It is at least unlikely that Harry Niemeyer will ever again walk up Bond Street or show his face in Milwaukee. He must rest on his laurels and be content with his European reputation.

. . . .

To give some idea of the actual difficulties of the final exit and escape, it may be well to include the following graphic account from the first man through (Butler);

"The kits of the first (working) party were got down in the daytime. I had been chosen to cut out, and as soon as the ten o'clock roll-call was over in the rooms,

Langren, Clouston, and I (we were going to 'travel' together) went off through the swing doors, the hole into the eaves, the orderlies' quarters, and so into the tunnel.

"I left my room at about 10.15 p.m., and in ten minutes I was worming my way along the hole for the last time, noting all the old familiar ups and downs and bends, bumping my head against the same old stones, and feeling the weight of responsibility rather much. I am not ashamed to say that I did a bit of praying on the way along. When I got to the end, into the small pit which we had dug to drop the earth of the roof into, I put my kit on one side and got to work with a large bread knife. It was of course pitch dark. I was kneeling in the pit, digging vertically up. The earth fell into my hair, eyes, and ears, and down my neck. I didn't notice it much then, but found afterwards that my shirt and vest were completely brown. By about 11 p.m. I had a hole through to the air about 6 inches in diameter. It was raining, but the arc lamps made it look very light outside. I found, to my delight, that we had estimated right and that I had come up just beyond a row of beans which would thus hide my exit, with any luck, from the sentry. By 11.40 the way was open, and I pushed my kit through and crawled out. The sentry nearest us had a cough, which enabled me to locate him, but as he was in the shadow of the wall and not in the light of the electric lamps I could not see him. This made it a bit more uncomfortable, as I didn't know but that he was staring straight at me. I crawled to the edge of the rye-field and looked at my watch. It was 11.45 p.m. Just at that moment the rain stopped, a bright full moon shone out and an absolute stillness reigned. The rye was very ripe and crackled badly, and so, after a whispered consultation with L., I decided to crawl in a southerly direction down the edge of the rye-field, keeping under cover of the gardens.

"If there had only been the three of us to escape we could have barged straight through the rye, but we had to think of the hordes behind us, and could not afford to take risks.

"We reached the end of the cover afforded by the gardens and were debating what to do, when luckily the rain started again, and we crawled through the rye, the noise of the rain pattering on the rye being sufficient to drown that made by our progress.

"When through the rye, we stopped to put on our rücksacks, and then made for the river Weser which we had to cross. Close to the river bank we found four or five large hurdles. Piling these one on top of the other, we made a raft, on which we ferried across first our kits and then our clothes. The water was warm, but the wind cold. We dressed and started again. It was by this time about 2 a.m. C. thought he heard a shot, and we were afraid that the Boche had spotted someone getting out.

"As we rounded the spur of a hill, and the lights of the *Lager*, which looked so pretty from outside, were shut from our view, we said good-bye to Holzminden *Kriegsgefangenenlager*—a good-bye which unhappily turned out for us three to be only 'au revoir.'"

. . . .

In all ten escaped. Rathborne, as stated, was over in three days, and was able to report in person on the state of affairs in one camp in the Xth Army Corps in which he had held a responsible position. Gray, Bain, Kennard, Bennett, and Bousfield among the working-party, Purves, Tullis, Campbell Martin, and Leggatt amongst the others, followed in the course of a fortnight. Most of them had had some near shaves and were " all in " on arrival. Bousfield—an old Cambridge 3-miler—had on one occasion to out-distance his pursuers by running for it.

Those who had been recaptured were kept in cells until early in September without trial, although repeated protests were made to the Commandant and higher authority. They were then released to await court-martial. The accused being many and rolling-stock being valuable, the Court came to Holzminden to judge them. On the morning of the trial a lawyer came to represent the prisoners, and a representative of the Netherlands minister at Berlin also came to act in their interests. All the prisoners were tried together and were sentenced to six months' imprisonment on a combined charge of mutiny and damage to property, the punishment to be carried out in a fortress. As it happened, and although the trial took place so early as 27th September, this sentence was never carried out. Whether this was due to the military situation or to some other cause is not known. The signing of the Armistice removed finally all possibility of the imprisonment ever being carried into effect.

It was unfortunate that while the Holzminden tunnel was under construction another tunnel was in progress at Clausthal, where the twin brother Niemeyer was Commandant. It is now known that the tunnel there would have been completed in about a week from the

Churchill

Clouston
Lyon

Bennett
Robertson Sharp Mardock

Group of recaptured officers in a room at Holzminden.

date on which the Holzminden escape took place. The "Poldhu" had been busy between the camps, but, no exact synchronisation being possible, it remained simply to go full steam ahead in each camp and trust to luck. As was anticipated, the Holzminden escape led to a very serious search at Clausthal, and the tunnel was discovered just as it was approaching completion. The tunnel of Holzminden was, however, so much the bigger affair that there was a rough justice in this award of Fortune.

CHAPTER XI

MAKING GOOD

THE officers' Lager at Stralsund lay on an island, or rather on a twin pair of islands, called Greater and Smaller Danholm, separated from the mainland by a narrow strip of water over which a permanent ferry plied to and fro. On the further side of these islands and separated from them again by a wider channel, perhaps two-thirds of the width of the Solent at its narrowest point, lay the pleasant shores of Rügen. The blue sea and the wooded slopes of this fair island recalled to the home-sick prisoner the beauties of her smaller sister of the Wight.

Hither in the summer of 1918 came 500 odd hungry British officers, the unwilling guests of his then Imperial Majesty Wilhelm II. They were a not inconsiderable part of the many taken in the three gigantic German offensives between March 21st and May 27th. They came in big batches from the sorting-out camps of Rastatt and Karlsruhe—the former place a memory that will endure for their lives with those who were there—or in little driblets from the hospitals whence they had been discharged.

Hither came also in September 200 officers from Aachen (Aix-la-Chapelle), the last of their illusions gone. They had been sent from various camps to that place, the stepping-stone for internment and happier things. They had stayed there two months. Their parcels,

which should have been forwarded to them, went per-
sistently "west." In many cases even their luggage had
gone to Holland. They had been taken for walks and
had viewed the promised land. And now, at the eleventh
hour, the congestion of sick at Aachen had necessitated
their removal and they had been side-tracked to the
Baltic—to wait and wait, and begin the dreary round
again. They moved our sympathy. They had had two
and a half years of it, and now they had as little to eat
as, and not much more to wear than, the new arrivals.
But one of them had a typewriter.

And hither came also a little party of three from
Holzminden Camp in Brunswick, transferred, as I have
previously explained, as suspected persons to a camp of
really reliable security. Major Gilbert, Lieutenant Ortweiler, and myself had been told one morning that we
had an hour and a half in which to pack. We packed
and went. Stralsund was like a rest cure.

It is indeed a pleasant spot. A channel, narrow at the
entrances, broadening to ninety yards in the middle,
divides the islands. Standing on the bridge which spans
the channel at its narrowest, one looks west to Stralsund
town. Whether with the setting sun behind it or with
the morning sun full on it, it is beautiful. Venice viewed
from the sea could hardly be prettier. The dome of
the Marianne Kirche dominates the town, and the bat-
coloured sails of the fishing vessels could be just seen,
with an occasional motor-boat, moving in the blue Sound.
In Greater Danholm the chestnuts are magnificent. There
is one avenue of trees which meet each other overhead
as in a cathedral nave. And there was one little segre-
gated, fenced-off spot which for no particular reason we

called King Henry VIIIth's Garden—the name seemed to suit. One could take half an hour walking round the camp.

But it is not my intention by painting too glowing a picture to alienate my reader's sympathy. The place was good, but German. The buildings were good, but had held Russians. The air was good, but there were smells. We had been long-time prisoners—veterans, we considered ourselves, in this horde of "eighteeners." And it would be cold, very cold in winter.

We had a fortnight's holiday, revelling in the unexpected beauty, the much less uncomfortable beds with their extra sheet, the open-air sea bath in the mornings, the freedom and scope of movement, the almost latent wire, the inoffensiveness of the German personnel, the unobtrusiveness of the Commandant, the beer (liquorice, but still beer of a sort), the exchange of news with the new prisoners and the picking up of old threads, the sight of the sea from our landing window, the games on real grass....

And then, in quite a different sense, we began looking round.

We learned that the authorities were quietly and politely confident that the place was escape-proof. They expected attempts. Oh! yes. "We know it is your duty. We should do it ourselves." And conventionalities of the sort that were common when German officers of a decent type—and there were such on this island—found themselves in conversation with Englishmen. "But it cannot be done—no one has ever escaped from here. True, it might be easy to cut the wire and get on to the main part of the island, but we have our dogs. If you swim to the mainland you will be recognised and brought back. Even if you get across to Rügen you have to get off it and you would be missed. We have our sea-plane to scour the sea. The ferry is guarded..." and so on.

Subsequent events appeared to justify this view. At-tempts were made, and failed in quick succession. In each case the objective was the same, though aimed at by different methods—the open sea and the Danish island of Bornholm or Danish territory elsewhere. Two officers, yachtsmen born, cut the wire one night, swam out towards Rügen, boarded an empty fishing vessel about 200 yards out and got clean away. They stranded off the north-west corner of Rügen and were recaptured. Three others commandeered a boat which had been left unpadlocked in the channel, rowed to the mainland, and separated. Two were recaptured immediately, the third was at large some days and was eventually arrested some way down the coast. I did not learn his story. Another party of three attempted to paddle over to Rügen on a cattle trough. They selected a stormy night, were upset fifty yards out of the channel, and got back, unobserved, with difficulty, and, as one of them could not swim, rather luckily.

So far as the German precautions went, the net upshot of these attempts was that stringent orders were issued about leaving boats in the channel or on the shores of the island unpadlocked. For the rest, the Commandant was satisfied with his second line of defence, the water, which was moreover (it was now mid-September) growing daily colder and more unattractive.

Such was the position when the Holzminden trio began

to put their heads together. I do not think any of us seriously entertained the idea of an escape by water. We were all hopeless landsmen, and Gilbert at any rate could not swim. A "stunt" by sea necessitated a combination of luck, pluck, opportunism, and, above all, watermanship. Our armament, such as it was, was of a different kind. We all knew German, Gilbert and I indifferently, Ortweiler fluently. We had the wherewithal to bribe. We could lay our hands on a typewriter. We knew the ropes of a land journey by railway. G. and O. had both been "out," the latter more than once; and I had heard these things much discussed. Moreover, Gilbert, being a Major, had secured a small room which he invited me to share, and Ortweiler was a member of our mess. In a deep-laid scheme privacy is almost an essential. Greatest asset of all, the Germans were not suspicious and they left us alone.

Our idea, very much in the rough, crystallised as follows: together or separately—as events might dictate—to bluff the sentry at the main gate, and at the ferry; to get on to the mainland and there travel by train to the Holland frontier; and to have our preparations so thoroughly made that, on paper at least, our plan was bound to be successful.

Our first idea was to co-opt three or four others and go out as a party of orderlies with one of us disguised as a German sentry in charge. Individual officers had on several occasions already been into the town with a party of orderlies on some "fatigue" or other in order to have a look round. Our idea was to concoct some imaginary fatigue which would take us not only into the town but out of it, where we should have an opportunity of

Facsimile of the original permit-card copied by Lockhead.

assuming our real disguise and separating on our respective routes. We got so far as to fashion out our bogus rifle in the rough, but before very long we discarded the whole idea for various reasons. The rifle would be too difficult to imitate to pass in broad daylight. We could not be certain of securing the uniform of our sentry; all the sentries on duty in the camp were likely to be personally known to one another. Difficulties of taking our disguise with us, difficulties of hitting on the right sort of "fatigue" to disarm suspicion...the "cons" had it emphatically.

Moreover, in the interval the looked-for "key" had presented itself. Gilbert had succeeded in removing a workman's "permit" from his coat pocket while he was working in the camp. This "permit" entitled the civilian in question to visit the camp and its environs between given dates, name and business being duly stated, and the permit signed by the Camp Commandant. Printed in German print on a plain white card, it appeared not impossible of exact imitation. Our hopes were more than fulfilled. Lieut. Lockhead, one of the party weatherbound en route for a neutral country, had, we knew, performed yeoman service in this line when at Holzminden. We showed him the card. Within two days he had accomplished an exact replica, including the signature, so good as to be undistinguishable from the original. Our hopes rose. It remained to complete the remainder of our essential equipment—civilian clothes, German money, forged passports, maps, and compasses. With the two former I was entirely unprovided. One passport, forged on an old model, was in Gilbert's possession, but we doubted its efficacy in northern Germany.

The two latter articles I was content to leave to the last moment, when I should have definitely decided on my route. One had the feeling that it was absurd to spend hours on acquiring articles necessary only for the last lap, when one might be stopped at the gate—a curiously illogical reasoning, as these things, or at least one of them, are indispensable for even a short journey across country...but there it was.

It was at this point that the event occurred which led me definitely to abandon my Holland scheme and decide for the Danish border. A German private soldier came into our room one day to do some work. He was in uniform but was on leave in Stralsund, which was his home, and in the then prevailing shortage of labour he was lending a hand to his erstwhile master.

No "escaper" ever omits a chance—provided he can speak German at all—of profiting by a conversation with someone from outside the camp. Indeed, this was so well known to the authorities that in most camps anybody coming in from outside was escorted by a sentry and not left alone during the period of his stay in the camp. Stralsund was an exception, possibly because the English had been there so short a time, possibly because of the Commandant's complacent idea as to its security. Be that as it may, I had this fellow fairly quickly sized up. It turned out his job was doing sentry on the Denmark border.

"Is it dull there?"

"Frightfully."

"Do many get over up there?"

"Oh yes."

"What? Prisoners?

"A few, but smugglers and deserters mostly. We pretend not to see them."

Here was an eye-opener! I threw caution to the winds and found that I had not mistaken my man. He was a genial rascal, venal and disloyal to the core. Before he had been in that room half an hour he had committed himself far too deeply in the eyes of the German law for me to have any fear that he would turn round and blow the gaff on *us*. He told us (Gilbert had come in by that time) of a slackly guarded frontier, with wire so low that you could walk over it; of the exact route from Stralsund to the last station outside the *Grenz-Gebiet* (border territory); of the innocuous passage of an ordinary *Personal-Zug* (slow train) without the complications of passport-checking or examination over the dreaded Kiel Canal. He came in next day with some civilian collars and ties and an inadequate railway map, and on each day he went out the heavier by sundry woollen and flannel clothes, cigarettes, soap, chocolate, and cheese. He gave me in return about 30 marks in German money. He had promised to do even more, but he made some excuse that his leave was up and we saw him no more. Probably he funked it. Viewed as a commercial deal, the balance was in his favour; but he had given us information that was beyond rubies. Our hopes rose higher, and by this time Gilbert and I were more or less definitely committed to the Denmark scheme.

We had not long to wait for an opportunity of seeing how our passports should read. I will say no more. Even at this distance of time, immeasurably magnified by the intervening events, there still may lurk the long arm in German law, and we need not doubt that there are still too many souls in Germany attracted by the thought: *Wie soll ich Detective werden?* (How shall I become a detective?) to make it altogether safe for those concerned if I were to be more explicit in print. Suffice it to say that our tools were of tender years, cheaply bought, and therefore on both accounts the less deserving of retribution[1]. I had sold my field service ration boots for 45 marks, through the agency of Ortweiler. I had therefore collected about 75 marks, and this was, of course, ample for my requirements. I was all the time anxiously on the look-out for civilian clothes. I had got a pair of old blue trousers from Captain Clarke of the Merchant Marine. I had an old pair of ration "Tommy" boots which on comparison with the home-grown article might just "do." I had shirt, collar, and tie. I wanted hat, coat, and, in view of the lateness of the season, some sort of overcoat.

By great good luck the hat, or, as it happened, cap, materialised. A new naval suit with cap had arrived for a merchant skipper who had gone to Aachen for a medical board with the hope of exchange. As soon as we had heard he had been passed and gone over the border, G. and I promptly closed for the suit, of which we had secured the refusal, with his *chargé d'affaires*. Shorn of its buttons the suit made a smart civilian costume for Gilbert, and shorn of its badge the cap became merely of the naval type of headgear so common amongst German boys or men of the working-class. I had always decided

---

[1] This chapter was written in 1918 and times have changed. We borrowed the passport off a glazier's boy who used to come into the camp. And we sold our boots to one of the camp canteen officials who was distinctly venal.

I would shape my rôle according to the clothes which I could find, and I now decided that I should travel 4th class, as some sort of mechanic. For a coat I had to fall back upon a brand new English coat sent out from home and confiscated by and restolen from the Germans. I made it as shabby as I could in the short time at my disposal but even so it was far too smart to pass for my class of "character" except at night. I therefore decided that if travelling by day I would wear over my coat a very old dark blue naval raincoat which had been given me. I was thus equipped. I might possibly have done better if I had waited, but the completion of my arrangements had to synchronise, as far as possible, with that of the others. I had also been able to copy a fairly good map of northern Schleswig, showing roads and railways, and, by great good luck and at the eleventh hour, I secured what I believe was the last compass but one in the whole camp. The shortage of these articles seemed extraordinary, when one reflected on the abundance of them in most of the old camps of longer standing. To the donor on this occasion I am eternally indebted, as I could not have managed very well without it.

From one of the camp personnel I had elucidated the fact that the Hamburg train went at 6.40 in the morning. From another source we heard there was also a train at 6.43 in the evening.

Gilbert meanwhile had been busy with the typewriter which he had secured with great forethought from its owner in the Aachen party. The "*Ausweis*" forms were completed, each according to our own particular specifications.

Mine ran as follows:

$$\left.\begin{array}{c}\textit{Personal-Ausweis}\\ \textit{für}\\ \textit{Karl Stein}\\ \textit{aus}\\ \textit{Stralsund}\end{array}\right\} \text{on the outside,}$$

and on the inside: on the left-hand side, my photograph —(I had been photographed in this very camp by the Germans and I had been wearing at the time an old Indian volunteer tunic which in the photograph looked much like a German tunic. This was pure chance and very lucky).

On the right side, my particulars:

Karl Stein.

Date of Birth:	4/6/1880.		
Place of birth:	Stralsund.		
State belonging to:	Prussian.	*Height:*	1.60 metres.
Chin:	Ordinary.	*Eyes:*	Brown.
Mouth:	Ordinary.	*Hair:*	Brown.
Nose:	Large.	*Beard:*	Moustache.
Particular marks:	None.		

Authentic Signature: Karl Stein.

(A very lame and halting hand this!)

"Herewith certified that the owner of the pass has subscribed his name with his own hand."

(*Signed*) Lieutenant of Police, Stralsund.

The stamps affixed to the passport—two on the photograph, one on the right-hand side—were an amazingly clever imitation by Lockhead (the friend who had already helped us with the forging of the permit-cards). He did these stamps by hand through some purple carbon paper that I still had with me from an old army message-form book, and to be believed they should be seen in the original.

1314

PERSONAL = AUSWEIS

für

Karl Stem

aus/ Stralsund

Vor= und Zunamen: _Karl Stein_

Geburtstag: _4. Juni 1880_

Geburtsort: _Stralsund_

Staatsangehörigkeit: _Preussen_

Grösse: _1,60._   Mund: _gewöhnlich_

Gestalt: _untersetzt_   Augen: _braun_

Kinn: _gewöhnlich_   Bart: _Schnurbart_

Nase: _gross_   Haare: _braun_

Besondere Kennzeichen: _____

Karl Stein
(Eigenhändige Unterschrift.)

    Es wird hiermit bescheinigt, dass
der Passinhaber vorstehende Unterschrift
eigenhändig vollzogen hat.

STRALSUND, den _1. Mai 1918_
DIE POLIZEI=SEKRETARIAT.
I.A.

G. took infinite trouble with the filling up of these passports. He had acquired a good flowing German hand and he filled the particulars in himself, with a flourish for the signature of the Police *Leutnant* at the bottom. He also filled in the permit-cards. We had each two passports, one made out as from Stralsund, and the other as from Schleswig. We should naturally show the Stralsund one in the Schleswig territory and *vice versâ*.

We were now ready, or as ready as anyone is until the actual time comes to go, when there are always a thousand and one things to be thought of.

.   .   .   .

It was arranged amongst ourselves that Ortweiler should have the first shot, as he stood easily the best chance of effecting escape. Accordingly, on Monday the 14th October he made his exit. He was well made up with a false moustache stuck on with some very diluted form of spirit gum, and fiercely curved at the tips. It was only tow, but it served its purpose in the dark. Our duty was to patrol the avenue leading to the main gate between 5 and 6.30 p.m., to mark down what dangerous Germans had left the camp, and to stop O. if anyone who was likely to suspect him hove in sight.

I should mention here that from the barrack selected as dressing room to the main gate is about 200 yards. From the main gate on to the ferry is another 350 yards. After dark at this time of year various Germans living in the town were likely to be leaving the island for the night, and the ferry was thus constantly on the move. Our object was primarily to avoid the more dangerous Germans, e.g. an officer or the Interpreter, who knew us all well by sight.

All went well. I gave the signal "all clear" at about

6.30 and G. and I piloted Ortweiler out, slowing down as he passed us 40 yards from the main gate. We saw him take out his card and hand it to the sentry, who then let him through the postern. It had worked! We breathed a sigh of relief. Just as we were going back, we met the Interpreter homeward bound for the ferry. He was too close behind O. to be exactly safe, so I engaged him in conversation. He was in a hurry and I could only think of something rather fatuous to say, but I held him up a minute or two and that may have caused him to miss Ortweiler's particular boat[1].

We "cooked" Ortweiler's *appel* at 8 p.m.—this is a familiar device for concealing escape. The result was that the barrack Feldwebel did not report his absence till next day at 9 a.m. roll-call. He had thus twelve hours' clear start, by which time he was most of the way to Berlin. We thought him almost a certainty to get over with his fluent knowledge of German, and he did, in point of fact, escape into Holland, *viâ* Berlin, Frankfort, and Crefeld, after a night's thrilling experience on the actual border which would be a story in itself[2].

G. and I were naturally elated, the more so as from enquiries it transpired that the authorities had absolutely no suspicion of how O. had got out. Owing to repeated wire-cutting and escapes into the island, the guard had been increased and placed outside the wire. No one had passed the sentries who had not the proper credentials. Of that they were quite convinced. It was believed that he was still hiding in the camp. We hugged ourselves.

Friday of that week, the 18th, the day selected as

[1] I have since heard that they went over the ferry together.

[2] Ortweiler came up to Cambridge but was killed shortly afterwards in a flying accident in Spain.

"*der Tag*," was an unforgettable one. Our kit had to be packed and labelled; final arrangements made about feeding in the event of recapture; compromising documents of any sort had to be destroyed; at the last moment I realised that I had no braces, no German cigarettes, and no matches. To crown all there was a barrack hockey match which we could not very well avoid.

During the day it so happened that we were twice invaded by Feldwebels. On the first occasion the door was locked and we had to throw a map into the corner and then open the door, an action which would in itself have been of damning suspicion in most camps. On the second, the Feldwebel found G. cutting sandwiches of German *Kriegs Brot* (war bread). G. had to explain that it was a new attempt to make *Kriegs Brot* palatable, and invited the Feldwebel to come and see the result at dinner time. Doubtless he came, but there were no sandwiches and no us. At 4 p.m. we had our high tea—four Copenhagen eggs each and tea and jam. At 5 p.m. the roll was called, and immediately after it we started transferring our disguise under cover of the growing darkness to the barrack from which we were going to make our final exit.

It had been arranged after some discussion that Gilbert should leave not before dark, and not later than 6, and that I should give him ten minutes clear before leaving. This would give me little time to catch the 6.42 train to Hamburg if I was at all held up (a forecast which was verified by events); but there was no help for it. It was necessary that Gilbert's disguise should be assisted to the full by darkness.

We had let a few friends into the secret and these were cruising about like destroyers up and down the avenue, reporting the departure of dangerous Germans. Gilbert did not eventually get off much before 6, and it seemed a long time before the leader of the convoy reported that G. was safely through the gate. I gave him ten minutes, conscious mainly of the fact that I had forgotten any German I had ever learnt, and then stepped forth.

I was Karl Stein, firm of Karl Stein & Co., Furniture Dealers, Langestrasse, Stralsund; I had been into the Kommandantur to arrange about a new contract for officers' cupboards. I knew the shop because I had seen it the day before when I went to the town hospital under escort with a party of officers for massage. I needed no massage, of course, but had only done this to acquaint myself with the geography of the town.

With a blank stare I passed several brother-officers walking up and down the avenue and reached the gate. My great moment had come, but the sentry simply looked at my card carefully, said *schön*, and handed it back. I walked very fast down to the ferry. There was no boat on my side and I saw I should have to wait some minutes. The sentry at the ferry examined my card and handed it back. How should I avoid the two Germans who were already there on the jetty waiting for the boat? I decided to have a violent fit of coughing.

I must here mention that my knowledge of German, acquired during captivity, was not such as would enable me to support a cross-examination of more than a minute or two. I had, however, practised the "pure" German accent with assiduity. In point of fact I hardly spoke a hundred words on the journey, and some of these were not absolutely necessary.

At last the ferry boat came over, empty. I got in and sat in the bows. There was an English orderly working the bow oar—I had seen him the previous day. I kicked him, and he realised what I was and shielded me as much as he could from the other occupants of the boat, which was now gradually filling. It was a long five minutes and I continued my violent fit of coughing, leaning over the side as if in a paroxysm. There were two Germans in the bows and one of them touched me on the shoulder and suggested that I should trim the boat by sitting in the middle. I complied meekly, feeling really very wretched indeed.

At the last I thought I was really done for. The German adjutant got into the boat. He didn't know me by sight, but I thought it was more than likely that he would suspect me. Mercifully he began to talk to some lady typists from the camp who had just preceded him.

We shoved off eventually, almost full. I continued coughing till we got across. When the boat discharged I went ashore almost last. I gave them a wide berth in front, and as soon as I was clear made off at my best pace for the station. Now I was Karl Stein of Schleswig, carpenter, ex-army man, and recalled for civilian employment, catching the train for his native country. I tore up my "permit" and dropped it in the road— one month off my sentence anyway.

As I expected, I just missed my train. I had no watch, but the clock on the Marianne Kirche showed me I should be late. I reached the station about 6.50; it was rather full of people. I wondered if Gilbert was away in that train... and then, vaguely, what the chances were of my being nabbed before the next went—this, I noted, was at 6.40 the next morning (Saturday). I think if there had been any outgoing trains that night I should have taken them, even though they led me east instead of west. But as it happened there were none. I went into the men's lavatory in the station, shut myself in a closet and reflected. I thought at that time to my horror that I had forgotten my matches, so I denied myself a smoke —my matches turned up later and I needed what few there were. I solaced myself with a slab of chocolate.

The position was not encouraging. Our information about trains was correct. Our friends would not be able to camouflage our absence, which would certainly be discovered by 8 p.m., reported by 9 p.m. It was more than likely that they would telephone to the station. I determined not to be in the station at all between 9 and 12. If I was arrested next morning, I was. In the meantime it was good to be free.

It was a beautiful October night in Stralsund. I braced myself up and begged a light for a cigarette from a youngster at a street corner, and then strolled along the streets that led from the station to the Kirche. I knew these now quite well enough not to get lost. I sat on a bench and looked across the moonlit water, which near the station runs right in in a broad and lovely sweep. I lit a pipe from my German cigarette and smoked comfortably. Should I get off next morning?...

I was cooling down now, and wandered down past the Marianne Kirche to a cinema in the Langestrasse. A boy there told me the booking office was shut. I wandered round and round till one o'clock. I sat for a long time on my old bench overlooking the water; at another place I entered a private garden and sheltered for an hour under a wall right on the water's edge. It was blowing fairly fresh.

About one o'clock I returned to the station and entered the waiting room, full of recumbent figures, mostly soldiers and sailors. I got hold of two chairs and tried to sleep. There was a sailor on the other side of the table.

At 4 o'clock I got up and had a cup of coffee. The waiting room was now fairly full of people, most of them presumably going by my train.

I had by now a two days' growth of beard and my moustache was fairly long and well down over the corners of my mouth. Moreover, I had had a fairly sleepless night.

In my pockets I carried three large sandwiches of German bread with English potted meat inside, about twenty slabs of Caley's marching chocolate, a box of Horlick's milk tablets, a spare pair of socks, some rag and vaseline, my pipe and tobacco, English and German cigarettes, my compass, money, and papers. I had an old German novel in my hands which I pretended to read with great assiduity. Half an hour before the train was due to start, I went to the booking office. I was surprised to hear my own voice. "Fourth to Hamburg, please." I had no idea what it cost, so I tendered a 20-mark note. The ticket cost only seven marks! I went back to the waiting room, and a few minutes later faced the barrier. No questions, no suspicion. I breathed again and wondered what that Commandant had done. Wired to Rostock perhaps....

My carriage was not over-full at the start—four or five women and two elderly men. I had no trouble with them. Their conversation began and maintained itself exclusively about food, but they were cheerful enough.

Before Rostock the carriage had filled up and I with British politeness was strap-hanging. An old woman began asking me to shift her *Korb* (basket). I could not exactly understand what she wanted and must have looked rather foolish. However, I did the right thing eventually.

We changed at Rostock. I was half expecting trouble but nothing happened. A porter told me the platform for the Hamburg train. I got this stereotyped question fairly pat.

To Hamburg the train was overflowing; we were over 40 in a tiny compartment. I was wedged in against the window, strap-hanging. At one intermediate station a young soldier got in with a goose hanging out of his haversack. He immediately became the centre of an admiring throng. He was a cheerful youth and bandied repartee with all and sundry—I could not catch his sallies, which were in low German and greeted with roars of laughter. I suppose he was the son of some farmer and had "wangled" this goose, which would probably have fetched 150 marks in the market, to take back to his mess-mates. He got out just before Hamburg. I could not have asked for a better foil.

Hamburg! I had never hoped for even so long a run as this. Was there really a chance?... In any case, I was now well clear of the Stralsund zone. I began to realise that the heavy week-end traffic was helping me and that I was indeed no more than a needle in a haystack. I ate a sandwich and an apple which I had bought at Lubeck.

We ran into the big station at about 2.40 in the afternoon—it was very full. It did not take me long to find the "departure" notices, Kiel 3.10. I took my place in the "queue" for the fourth class booking office. Behind me two women had an altercation as to priority of place in the "queue." I was rather afraid they were going to appeal to me. I had no wish for the rôle of Solomon at that moment.

I booked direct to Flensburg—about four marks' worth —and made my way downstairs to the departure platform, which was indicated clearly enough. I did not like the odd quarter of an hour which I had to wait before the train came in. I was not very happy about my dark blue waterproof. I could not see anything approaching its counterpart. If one stands still, one can be examined at leisure ; if one moves up and down, one runs the gauntlet of a hundred restless eyes, any one pair of which may at some previous date have had first hand cognisance of a typical naval rubber-lined English waterproof....

Then I blundered. There was a coffee-stall on the platform. I went up to it and asked for a cup. I had drunk nothing since 4 o'clock in the morning. Fortunately neither of the *Frauleins* in the stall paid any attention to me. Just then I saw the notice "*for soldiers and sailors only*" printed up in big letters. I should have known that, but no one had noticed anything.

When *would* that train come in?

It came at last. I chose the carriage with fewest soldiers in it, and most women, and made for my strategical position by the window. But it was impossible to avoid men altogether. I had one strap-hanging next to me from Hamburg to Kiel. Everybody started chattering at once. How could I keep out of this all the way to Kiel without suspicion? Of course, they were talking about food—various ways of dishing up potatoes.

I looked out of the window, pretending to be interested in the country. It was impossible even to pretend to read in that crush. A man on the seat was forcibly expressing his views to two *Frauleins* on the new (10th) War Loan. They giggled.

I often wonder if those Hamburg folk then had any notion that another fortnight would see the Red Flag floating in their midst.

At Neumünster we had an invasion. The carriage, full already, became packed. Four girls of the farmer class—sisters, I judged them—got in at my window. I lost my place of vantage and was relegated to the middle of the floor. I felt a pasty-faced youth quite close to me sizing me up....

Fortunately the farmer girls riveted all attention for half a dozen stations. They were in boisterous spirits and screamed with laughter at their own jokes. They spoke dialect and I could not understand them, but I grinned feebly in unison. When they got out, I recovered my post by the window. Bless them, anyway, for a diversion.

At the next station an elderly man who was sitting on a basket immediately in front of me said something to me directly. He was not in any way a formidable character, but he spoke villainous dialect and I could not make head or tail of his question. He was referring to something in the station. I said *Ja* and looked out of the window in a knowing way. But I could not risk a second question. I felt the pasty-faced youth's eyes on me again, and I made a bee-line for the lavatory. When I emerged I took up a fresh position.

The train was emptying as we approached Kiel, and

for a time I got my head out of the window and enjoyed the draught. Then a little girl standing by me asked me to pull up the window again. I had my second sandwich.

We ran into Kiel at about 6 o'clock. There was no difficulty. A guard, in answer to my question, pointed at the Flensburg train. The carriage I got into was not lit at all and almost empty. What a relief to sit! A girl came in to check my ticket, and I went to sleep. We went over the canal in the dark. There were two men in my carriage. I woke up at some wayside station and asked if it was Flensburg. They laughed and said Flensburg was two hours away yet. I muttered sleepily that I was a stranger, and pretended to drop off again.

I reached Flensburg about 10.30 p.m., and thought of the unforgettable scene in *The Riddle of the Sands*. I was no less depressed than Carruthers on that occasion. I was very thirsty, but it was a poky little station and there was nothing in the shape of a waiting room or coffee-stall. I lingered on the platform and saw a porter who appeared to be closing down for the night. I asked him what time the train to Tondern went next day. He first said 6 o'clock, but then reflected that the next day was Sunday and there would not be a train till eleven. He added that the train went from the other station. So there were two stations in Flensburg! My sentry friend had not told me this. I asked him where the other station was and he directed me. My German at this juncture was so abominable that I think he must have been a Dane.

At the other station, which I found to be the main one, there was a fairly large crowd in the booking hall.

They were waiting for the in-coming 11 o'clock train from the north. Entry to the platform and waiting rooms was barred. The train came in, the crowd dissolved, and the station was shut up for the night. I had got to put in twelve dreary hours in this place.

I took risks that night in Flensburg, risks that might have been fatal further south. I argued that here if anywhere one might expect to find a scrubby-faced man with a nautical cap and overcoat. I walked for about an hour past the quays, past the two main hotels, then up towards the church and down again to the quays. I could find no public drinking-fountain, which was what I was looking for, but I had learned the rough geography of the place.

There was a low barrier leading on to one of the quays. The gate was locked but I climbed the barrier and sat down on a bench. Behind me was one of those pavilions such as are seen on an English pier-head; in front, a steamer moored alongside. Both were quite deserted. Here at least I could sit and find solitude.

I took off my boots and attended to one of my toes which I had rubbed playing hockey the day before—what weeks ago it seemed! I went through my pockets and—joy!—found my matches. I smoked a luxurious pipe. Then, still in my socks, I boarded the steamer and searched her for water without success. She was fitted up for passengers and for a moment I entertained the idea of stowing myself away on her.

Just as I had finished putting on my boots again a man—a night-watchman I suppose he was—came on to the quay from the left. He must have been attracted by some movement. I confess I thought it was all up.

"What are you doing here?"

"Nothing."

"But you have no business to be here at all."

Silence implied assent. He beckoned me after him. He was not a Prussian, this man, whatever else he was. Perhaps he was afraid of me. He appeared to be taking me into some form of building on my right. I pretended to be coming along after him, but I swerved to the right, scrambled over the barrier and ran for 200 yards down the street. Fortunately there was no one about. I was not followed. I was thankful I had got my boots on in time.

I passed the first hotel and saw a woman with a man carrying her bag go in and ask for a room. She got one. I followed in after her and asked for a bed. The proprietor said he was full up and shut the door in my face. Could a two days' growth of beard make such a difference in a man? I was rather hurt.

But worse was to follow. I entered another hotel and saw some German sailors being given the keys of their bedrooms by a Fraulein. I asked her for some coffee. "No." "Water?" "No." "Nothing to drink?" "No, nothing."

I came to my senses and fled....

I went up towards the church, which stands on the top of a steep hill. There are some gardens sloping down the hill. I found an old sort of summer-house in one of these and went to sleep. It was about 1 a.m., and none too warm.

I was up at dawn and started again on my weary pilgrimage of the streets of Flensburg. How I hated that place! I half thought of altering my plan and doing the rest of the journey on foot. It was about 70 kilometres to the frontier.

I passed three military policemen in half an hour and wondered resentfully what they were doing in such large quantities on a *Sunday* morning.

At about eight I got to the station, and ate my last sandwich. Assuming that the porter had been right the previous night, I had got to put in three hours more dreary waiting. There were no overhead notices, but I noticed a useful-looking collection of time-tables stuck up on big boards in a little alcove just out of the booking hall. If I could get behind the rearmost of these I could put in much of my time unobserved. People might come and people might go, but they would never dream that I had been there all the time.

I examined the time-tables. I could make nothing of the Sunday trains, but I found the name Ober-Jersthal. That had been the station given by our informant at Stralsund as the last station outside the *Grenz-Gebiet*. In the maps we had seen in the camp we had never been able to verify this place. Ober-Jersthal must be on the main line running up the east Schleswig coast. So far so good, but at what time would this train go? It could not be the same train as the Tondern train, for Tondern is west Schleswig.

I wandered on to the platform. The bookstall was open and I bought a paper and also a Pocket Railway Guide. The Guide had a good map. I saw from this that the Tondern and Ober-Jersthal lines branched off at Tingleff—possibly the two trains went in one as far as Tingleff. I had not long to wait for corroboration. At the cloak-room I heard a man ask the attendant what

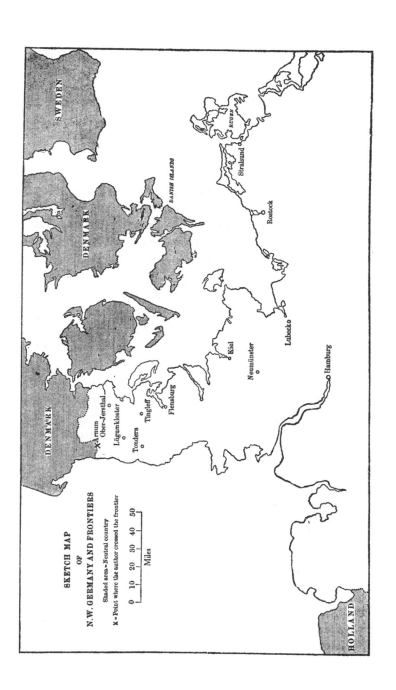

SKETCH MAP
OF
N.W. GERMANY AND FRONTIERS

Shaded area=Neutral country

× = Point where the author crossed the frontier

0 10 20 30 40 50
Miles

time the train went for a station which I knew to be north of Ober-Jersthal on the same line. The answer was 11.3. There could be no doubt of it now. I booked for Ober-Jersthal.

I had still an hour to wait. It passed somehow. I went into the waiting room and got my first drink for 29 hours, a glass of beer; it was washy stuff but went down wonderfully well. There were a lot of *Matrosen* (sailors) in the waiting room. Some of them stared at me and I began to have the Hamburg platform haunted sensation over again. I pretended to read my paper fiercely for half an hour and then went on to the platform. I began to regret that I had not had a shave that morning.

The train came in punctually. There was no incident till Tingleff, about 20 kilos northward. There I saw the passport officials waiting on the platform. I had almost forgotten about this part of the business....

I took a sudden resolution and left the train. I reckoned that I had not more than 40 miles to walk from this point, and by alighting here I might dodge the passport men altogether. But I was undeceived. An official was waiting at the entrance to the sub-way. He looked an easy-going fellow and was engaged in conversation with someone. He took my passport, glanced at it, and handed it back without a word. He did not even look to compare my face with the photograph. The great moment which Gilbert and I had rehearsed countless times had come and gone.

I hurried through the sub-way, and saw another passport official talking to the ticket collector. I handed in my Ober-Jersthal ticket. The man looked up in some surprise, but I was ready for him:

"I have shortened my journey."

"*Ach! So.*"

He asked no more questions. If he had, I doubt if I could have answered them. I was conscious only of one great wish, to be rid of the railway for good. I struck due north out of the station and found myself in a *cul-de-sac*. I was so overjoyed to be quit of the rail that I plunged into the fields. I had not gone very far before I had reason to repent. There was water everywhere, and I made very heavy weather of it. My objective was Lügumkloster, about 20 miles north-west from Tingleff, and I reckoned that it could not be very long before I struck the main road. After about two hours—it was now two o'clock in the afternoon—I found the road. There were very few people about, and those I met gave me good day civilly enough. If questioned at this point, I was going to have been a South German staying with relatives in Flensburg and out for a cross-country ramble—an improbable enough story.

My hopes had risen and it all seemed reasonably plain sailing now. The people were not suspicious. I had my map with a few important names...my compass...I might even do it in the next night.

I wondered exactly where old Gilbert was at this moment. It never even occurred to me that he had been caught, but such, as afterwards transpired, must have been the case[1].

Passing through one village I met some French prisoners. I gave them good day and told them who

[1] Gilbert had been caught actually on the border the night before, under the impression that he was already in Denmark. He was thought at first to be a smuggler!

I was. They invited me to come into their room in the farm where they were working. They were able to tell me what village I was in, Dollderup, and this was a great assistance. I thanked them in execrable French, gave them one of my remaining cigarettes, and told them what news I could—they had heard nothing for months. I don't think anything on the whole journey was more difficult than framing those few simple French sentences.

The signposts made the journey easy after that. At 3 p.m. I had 18 kilometres to go to Lügumkloster. I turned off the road, lay down in some young fir trees, took off my boots, ate some chocolate, and had half an hour or more's sleep.

I started again towards dusk. I was feeling very fit now and full of hope. If only I didn't muck it on the frontier....

The signposts did their duty nobly. There was a keen wind from the north and the road was good. I had been out just two complete days.

In one village a soldier with a rifle came out of a house just as I passed it. He replied to my " *Guten Abend* " courteously.

I reached Lügumkloster, I suppose, about half-past nine or ten. It is a big rambling village, and I made a bad mistake here on leaving it. I meant to take the Arrip-Arnum road, which runs roughly north-east. I took a road running north-east, but after about an hour's walking I found it was leading me gradually more east than north—I had not noticed that the wind had shifted from north to east. I decided to leave the road and make due north on the compass, trusting to pick up the right road later on. Then began a trying time.

The ground was terribly wet and intersected with continual wired ditches. I tore my clothes rather badly here and I don't think my trousers at the end of my journey would have stood another rip. However, I kept due north, tacking as little as possible to avoid the ditches, and eventually reached the road. It was, I supposed, about 2 a.m. I estimated I was still quite ten miles from the frontier. There was a strong wind, and I had not enough matches to spare to look more than once or twice at my map. Added to this, the signposts, previously so well-behaved, became infuriating. They only mentioned names which I had never heard of, or at least had not committed to memory.

Slog! Slog! Slog! I was getting tired. A man passed me with a cart. What on earth did *he* think he was doing at that time of night?

There was lots of water about and I did not go thirsty. My cap made an effective cup.

A light railway running parallel to the road—this was the *Klein Bahn* (light railway) the fellow had told us of.

Slog! Slog! Sl—. What on earth was that? A sentry box on the roadside, and in the box a sentry yawning and stretching himself. On each side of the road a belt of barbed wire running east and west.

I took these things in vaguely, disconnectedly. Had I miscalculated and was I over the border after all? He hadn't even challenged....

A mile later I crawled into a little hollow by the roadside to rest and get warm. I was getting strangely lightheaded. I remember addressing myself as a separate entity. I pulled myself together and sat down to think.

"I must go back and have another look at that wire. It can only be a protective belt for military purposes."

I went back. The wire was there sure enough. So was the sentry box, but I didn't go up to it. The wire was like the rear defence lines one had seen in France.

I retraced my steps. I still had the idea of picking myself up from the hollow where I had left myself.

I continued my way, praying for the night to end. With the dawn, I felt I should be able to think clearly again.

"Arnum 4 kilometres." The signposts were German enough, anyway.

Arnum, I had made out from my map, lay about three or four kilometres away from the point of the salient where I meant to cross the border. It was nearly dawn and I saw that I could not get over that night.

It was getting light as I reached the village. I left the road and struck west across the fields, up on to some high ground.

Somewhere in front there was Denmark.

I chose a hiding place in some young firs and heather. I was sheltered from the wind and was fairly comfortable.

One more whole day! What an age it seemed! I got out my railway map and looked at my position. I could not be more than five or six kilometres from the frontier. Somewhere in the valley to the north-west stretched the line of sentries. I decided to sally forth while it was still light in the late afternoon, take my bearings, and go over at dark.

As I lay there I heard footsteps. A boy came by

singing and passed within two yards of me. He didn't
see me. Just as well perhaps....

I took off my boots, rubbed my feet down, and had
some chocolate.

About noon it started raining and went on for about
three hours. I got wet through, but welcomed the rain
on the whole as it would get darker sooner.

I was now thinking quite connectedly, and, it being
impossible to sleep, I went over in my mind again and
again what I meant to do, and what I knew already about
the frontier.

I suppose it was about 5 when I started out. I reckoned
there would be about one more hour's daylight. I steered
due north-west across fields and marsh land for about
three kilometres. Suddenly, to my right—about 400
yards off—the sentries' boxes came full in view. There
was no mistaking them, about 200 yards between
most of them, and quite 300 yards between the two
opposite me.

I plumped down in the heather where I was standing,
and watched them. I saw a sentry leave his box and
walk about 20 yards up and down. I could see nothing
that looked like wire. Only marsh and heather in between....

Looking from where I was into Denmark, there was
a farmhouse immediately between the two sentry boxes.
I could take my course on that—it would be silhouetted
long after dark.

I waited till it was quite dark, and then started off,
taking no risks—crawling. I came to a ditch with wire
on each side of it. This was the only wire I saw. When
I judged I was well through the line, I got up and walked

to the farmhouse. A tall figure answered my knock. I began in my best German....

He shook his head to indicate that he didn't understand. I could have kissed him.

At last we hammered it out.

"*Engelsk Offizier. Fangen. Gut.*"

He beckoned me in with beaming face.

I had made good in just 72 hours. Beginners' luck!

EPILOGUE

THAT must remain in my memory as the greatest moment of my life. I had made good. Nor did I know that by the time I arrived in England it would all be over bar the shouting.

The old boy took me inside. He was a widower and I shared his simple fare. I remember honey and some sort of oat-cake that made my throat very sore. He had much less German than I and how we carried on a conversation till bed-time is more than I can remember.

I slept on a bed of straw in the cow-stall in under-clothing provided by my host, and the noise which the beasts made only woke me to pleasant reality.

Next morning we jogged in his cart over heath country into Ribe, a pretty old cathedral town. My farmer friend quickly let it be known what I was and I became an object of friendly interest in the market-place. But I little realised when I parted with him that I was at the same time again surrendering my freedom. For two days I was to be the victim of the quarantine regulations of the place. Politely but firmly I was sent to bed.

Being sent to bed when you are perfectly well and have a reasonable desire to exercise the privileges of freedom is a tedious business and I fear that I was lacking in cordiality to the buxom lady who attended on me and would have (but there I was firm) washed me. But I was allowed to send a telegram home, had plenty of English papers to read, and conversed through the window with the very friendly American Consul of the place.

When at last I was fumigated to the satisfaction of the authorities the American did all that lay in his power to make things pleasant for me. He entertained me at the principal hotel, rigged me out in a civilian suit, put me in funds and arranged for my early removal.

I remember only dimly the rail journey over the Jutland plain and the train ferry on the way to Copenhagen, where I was dined and boarded by the Minister. (Only the glass and the napery and the general Englishness of that table stand out in my memory.) The next day I saw the British Consul and sent a polite telegram to Niemeyer. I hope it reached him. Thereafter I remember only the long train journey to Bergen broken by one night at Christiania, myself now only one of many English fellow travellers coming from Heaven knows where on the King's business or their own to make the passage of the North Sea. I remember two wet days at Bergen and the relief of getting on board the "Juppiter" for the final stage. It was very rough and we were "hove to" for several hours and finally put in for shelter at Lerwick in the Shetlands. There I shared the privilege with two other exalted personages of going ashore and being entertained by Admiral Greatorex. A fishing expedition organised for our benefit on the chance of a late sea trout still offering was a failure for no line could have stayed on the water in that wind. When we finally put out from Lerwick on the last stage I remember my anxiety on the score of mines, ours or German. It was weather to unhook any mine from its fastenings and I was by now feeling too home- and sea-sick not to magnify possibilities. It was obvious that unescorted and in that sea we should have had no chance had we struck one.

But all went well and we landed at Aberdeen on the 8th November to hear the news of the Austrian capitulation. The next morning I was home. My repatriation had taken nearly three weeks.

I delayed reporting till after the week-end. On the morning of the 11th November I went up to London and by the time that I reached the War Office the war had come to an end, and returned prisoner stock was at a discount. But I did learn there that not a few compasses had been secreted in my parcels to Holzminden which accounted in some measure for Niemeyer's anxiety to get rid of me.

By an odd chance when I dropped into Cox's Bank about a month or six weeks later I met many of the Holzminden brigade just repatriated. Even then they had not freed themselves from the "queue" habit but this time it was to cash sterling cheques.